SPLITTING-UP PRECEDENTS

AUSTRALIA
LBC Information Services
Sydney

CANADA and USA
Carswell
Toronto

NEW ZEALAND
Brooker's
Auckland

SINGAPORE and MALAYSIA
Thomson Information (S.E. Asia)
Singapore

SPLITTING-UP PRECEDENTS

By

JACQUI JACKSON
Solicitor,
Legal Director of the
Solicitors' Family Law Association

LONDON
SWEET & MAXWELL
1998

Published in 1998 by Sweet & Maxwell Limited
100 Avenue Road
London NW3 3PF
(http://www.smlawpub.co.uk)

Computerset by LBJ Typesetting Ltd of Kingsclere
Printed and bound in Great Britain by Butler and Tanner Ltd, Frome and London

No natural forests were destroyed to make this product;
only farmed timber was used and re-planted.

ISBN 0–421–583 606

A CIP catalogue record for this book is available
from the British Library

All rights reserved. U.K. statutory material is
acknowledged as being Crown copyright.

No part of this publication may be reproduced or transmitted in any form or by any means, or stored in any retrieval system of any nature without prior written permission, except for permitted fair dealing under the Copyright, Designs and Patents Act 1988, or in accordance with the terms of a licence issued by the Copyright Licensing Agency in respect of photocopying and/or reprographic reproduction. Application for permission for other use of copyright material including permission to reproduce extracts in other published works shall be made to the publishers. Full acknowledgment of author, publisher and source must be given.

©
Jacqueline Jackson
1998

CONTENTS

Introduction	xi
Table of Cases	xv
Table of Statutes	xvii
Table of Statutory Instruments	xix

PART I
ACTIONS RELATING TO PROPERTY—OWNERSHIP OR OCCUPATION

A. APPLICATION FOR AN ORDER FOR SALE AND/OR DETERMINATION OF BENEFICIAL INTERESTS

The Law	1
The Procedure	4
The Precedents:	9
A1. Originating Summons for Order for Sale and/or Declaration of Beneficial Interests	9
A2. Originating Application for Order for Sale and/or Declaration of Beneficial Interests	11
A3. Affidavit in Support of Order for Sale	12
A4. Affidavit in Reply to Order for Sale	14
A5. Affidavit in Support of Declaration as to Beneficial Ownership and Order for Sale	15
A6. Affidavit in Reply to Declaration as to Beneficial Ownership and Order for Sale	17
A7. Notice to a Person Not a Party who will or may be affected by any Judgment	19
A8. Notice of Appointment to Hear Summons	20
A9. Order Declaring Beneficial Ownership and Ordering Sale	21
A10. Notice of Judgment to Person Not a Party who may be affected by it	23
A11. Summons for Declaration as to Beneficial Interest in Deposit Account or in Contents and Order for Sale	24

B. POSSESSION PROCEEDINGS

The Law	26
The Procedure	26
The Precedents	28
B1. Summons for Possession	28
B2. County Court Claim for Possession	30
B3. Originating Summons for Declaration by Licencee that his/her Licence has not been Terminated	31
B4. Defence by Licencee Denying Termination of Licence	32
B5. Order for Possession	33

C. APPLICATION UNDER SECTION 17 OF THE MARRIED WOMENS PROPERTY ACT 1882

The Law	35
The Procedure	35
The Precedents	37
C1. Originating Summons	37
C2. Affidavit in Support	39
C3. Affidavit in Answer	41
C4. Order	43

D. APPLICATION TO ENFORCE COHABITATION CONTRACTS OR SEPARATION DEEDS

The Law	44
The Procedure	44
The Precedents	46
D1. Action to Enforce Covenants in a Cohabitation Contract	46
D2. Defence	48
D3. Action to Enforce Covenants in a Separation Deed	49
D4. Defence	50
D5. Order for Specific Performance	51

E. ACTIONS UNDER SCHEDULE 1 OF THE CHILDREN ACT 1989

The Law	52
The Procedure	52
The Precedents	53
E1. Form C1	53
E2. Form C6	53
E3. Form C6A	53
E4. Form C7	53
E5. Form C9	53
E6. Form C10	53
E7. Form C10A	53

PART II

ACTIONS BY A SURVIVOR WHEN ONE PARTNER DIES

A. CLAIMS UNDER THE INHERITANCE (PROVISION FOR FAMILY AND DEPENDANTS) ACT 1975

The Law	55
The Procedure	56
The Precedents	59
A1. Originating Summons	59
A2. Affidavit in Support	61
A3. Affidavit in Answer	63
A4. Order Extending Time	65
A5. Interim Order	66
A6. Order	67

B. ACTIONS TO RESOLVE DISPUTED SUCCESSION TO PRIVATE TENANCIES

The Law	68
The Procedure	68
The Precedents	70
B1. Originating Application to Ascertain Tenant on Death of Former Tenant	70
B2. Affidavit in Support	71
B3. Order Determining Tenancy	73

C. APPLICATIONS FOR A BENEFICIAL INTEREST AND/OR ORDER FOR SALE   73

D. ACTIONS TO RESOLVE DISPUTES ABOUT GUARDIANSHIP

The Law	75
The Procedure	75
The Precedents	76
D1. Form C1	76
D2. Form C2	76
D3. Form C6	76
D4. Form C6A	76
D5. Form C9	76
D6. Form C46	76

E. FATAL ACCIDENTS ACT 1976 APPLICATIONS

The Law	77
The Procedure	77

The Precedents 79
    E1. Particulars of Claim 79

PART III

ACTIONS RELATING TO CHILDREN

A. ACTIONS TO RESOLVE DISPUTES ABOUT PATERNITY

The Law 81
The Procedure 82
The Precedents 85
    A1. Petition for Declaration as to Parentage 85
    A2. Affidavit Verifying Facts in Petition 87
    A3. Declaration of Parentage 88

B. APPLICATIONS FOR PARENTAL RESPONSIBILITY ORDERS

The Law 89
The Procedure 90
The Precedents 91

C. APPLICATION FOR DISCHARGE OF A PARENTAL RESPONSIBILITY ORDER OR AGREEMENT

The Law 92
The Procedure 92

D. APPLICATIONS FOR AN ORDER UNDER SECTION 8 OF THE CHILDREN ACT 1989

The Law 93
The Procedure 94
The Precedents 95

E. APPLICATION TO CHANGE CHILD'S NAME OR REMOVE FROM THE UNITED KINGDOM

The Law 96
The Procedure 96

F. APPLICATION FOR AN ADOPTION ORDER

The Law 97
The Procedure 98
The Precedents 100
    F1. Originating Summons or Originating Application 100
    F2. Agreement to Adoption Order 106
    F3. Notice of Hearing 109

F4. Notice of Intention to Apply to Dispense with Agreement	111
F5. Statement of Facts	112
F6. Interim Order for Adoption	113
F7. Abridged Adoption Order	114

G. APPLICATION FOR FINANCIAL PROVISION

The Law	116
The Procedure	117
The Precedents	118
G1. Form C1	118
G2. Form C2	118
G3. Form C6	118
G4. Form C6A	118
G5. Form C7	118
G6. Form C9	118
G7. Form C10	118
G8. Form C10A	118

PART IV

ACTIONS FOR PROTECTION FROM DOMESTIC VIOLENCE

A. APPLICATIONS UNDER PART IV OF THE FAMILY LAW ACT 1996

The Law	119
The Procedure	127
The Precedents	133
A1. Application for an Order	133
A2. Affidavit in Support	133
A3. Statement of Service	136
A4. Injunction Order	136
A5. Application to Vary, Extend or Discharge	136
A6. Power of Arrest	136
A7. Application for Warrant of Arrest	136
A8. Affidavit in Support of Application for Warrant of Arrest	137
A9. Warrant of Arrest	139
A10. Notice to Mortgagees and Landlords	139
A11. Transfer of Proceedings	139
A12. Supplement for an Application for an Emergency Protection Order	139
A13. Emergency Protection Order	139
A14. Interim Care Order	139

B. APPLICATIONS IN TORT

The Law	140
The Procedure	140
The Precedents	142
B1. Particulars of Claim	142
B2. Application for Injunction	143

C. PROTECTION FROM HARASSMENT ACT 1997

The Law	144
The Procedure	145
The Precedents	145

PART V
NON-CONTENTIOUS DOCUMENTS

A. SEPARATION AGREEMENT	147
B. TRANSFER FROM JOINT NAMES INTO SOLE NAME	149
C. ASSIGNMENT OF TENANCY WITH LANDLORD'S CONSENT	150
D. CHANGE OF NAME	151
E. APPOINTMENT OF TESTAMENTARY GUARDIAN	153
F. APPLICATION UNDER THE CRIMINAL INJURIES COMPENSATION SCHEME	154

APPENDICES — 155

1. Standard Forms	157
2. Checklist for Part 1—Property Disputes	221
3. Flowchart for Beneficial Interests	224
Flowchart for Occupation Orders—Part IV Family Law Act 1996	225

Index   227

INTRODUCTION

This book attempts to bring together within one cover all the forms of action which a person who has been living with someone else might require when that cohabitation comes to an end—whether because the relationship has broken down or because one cohabitant has died. Unmarried couples have no automatic rights arising from simply living together and so, in the absence of any agreement between them, they have to prove entitlement through the courts. This is so whether they are trying to establish a beneficial interest in a property or a right to occupy that property, a right to inherit on their partner's death or a right to share parental responsibility for a child. Difficulties may arise between cohabitants who are not living together as husband and wife such as couples of the same sex, friends or relatives living together. They too will have to prove entitlement through the courts to an interest in real or personal property or a right to occupy.

A married couple may separate after a day or a week but are still entitled to seek the discretion of the court in adjusting property and financial matters between them, entitled to inherit on the spouse's death and share parental responsibility. An unmarried couple may live together for thirty years and never acquire those rights.

There has been much talk about the injustices created by such a system. In *Burns v. Burns* [1984] Ch. 317 Fox L.J. said "... she lived with him for 18 years as man and wife, and, at the end of it, has no right against him. But the unfairness of that is not a matter which the courts can control. It is a matter for Parliament". In *Fitzpatrick v. Sterling Housing Association Ltd, The Times,* July 31, 1997, Lord Justice Waite said that the willingness to treat heterosexual cohabitants as if they were husband and wife for the purposes of succession to a statutory tenancy "was a restrictive extension offensive to social justice and tolerance because it excluded lesbians and gays". However one has also to consider the interests of property owners and "The task of reconciling the conflicting interests was better suited to the legislative function of Parliament than to the interpretative role of the courts".

In 1979 the Law Commission stated that it might be appropriate to reform the law governing contracts between couples living together. In the absence of any such reform, Teresa Gorman M.P. laid a bill before Parliament in 1991 to clarify the enforceability of cohabitation contracts but it was not considered necessary. The situation regarding enforcement remains unclear to a lot of people. In 1994 the Law Commission stated that it was to look at the property rights of home sharers and what should happen if the relationship breaks down. A report is still awaited.

In the meantime, cohabitants and their lawyers have to find their way round a myriad of different remedies and forms of relief. The lawyers have to carry out extensive enquiries before being able to advise on the appropriate form of relief. Does the client have a beneficial interest in a property? If so, is the size of it expressly defined? If not, what were the arrangements between the parties? Can an agreement to share the beneficial interest be implied? What contributions were made? Was any inducement or encouragement given? How long did they live together? Did they live together as husband and wife?, etc. It is hoped that this book will help practitioners by providing all the options, in one place.

The book is divided into five parts. Each of the first four parts is set out in a similar way. For each form of relief, there are three sections. The first gives a brief description of the law, the second describes the procedure and the third contains precedents to be used in such an action. The section on the law is intended to give the practitioner a short reminder of the basis on which an action can be brought and to set the procedure and precedents in context. It is not intended to be a comprehensive treatise on the subject. The precedents include affidavits where appropriate and these contain fictional situations to give the reader an idea of the sort of matters to include.

In Part III (Actions Relating to Children), the precedents are Children Act forms and so are not reproduced for each form of relief. Part V sets out some precedents for non-contentious documents which might be useful and so there is no description of the law and procedure there.

Part I deals with actions relating to property because the property is often the largest investment people make together and it also provides a home and so a great deal will be at stake. It deals with issues of ownership and occupation.

Part II deals with actions by a survivor when one partner dies. It includes claims where the survivor is not provided for or not adequately provided for in a will or by the rules of intestacy, actions to resolve disputes about tenancies and about guardianship and Fatal Accidents Act claims.

Part III deals with actions relating to children including issues of paternity, parental responsibility, residence and contact, changing the name, adoption and financial provision.

Part IV deals with actions for protection from domestic violence under Part IV of the Family Law Act 1996 effective from October 1, 1997 and looks briefly at the possibility of actions in tort or under the Protection from Harassment Act 1997.

Part V is made up of non-contentious documents which might be useful where agreement has been reached between the parties such as a separation agreement, transfer of property or tenancy. I would like to thank Frances Lees for her assistance with the transfer.

The Appendices contains a checklist and flowcharts to assist practitioners when taking instructions and deciding what action to take and the standard forms.

It is hoped that this format will be of practical help to practitioners. Any constructive comment on the content or lay-out would be appreciated.

TABLE OF CASES

A (A Minor) (Paternity: Refusal of Blood Test), Re [1994] 2 F.L.R. 463; [1994] Fam. Law 622, CA. 3–01

Bernard v. Josephs [1982] Ch. 391; [1982] 2 W.L.R. 1052; (1982) 126 S.J. 361; [1982] 3 All E.R. 162; (1983) 4 F.L.R. 178... 1–08
Bishop v. Plumley [1991] 1 W.L.R. 582; [1991] 1 All E.R. 236; [1991] 1 F.L.R. 121; [1991] Fam. Law 61; (1990) 140 N.L.J. 1153; *The Independent*, June 29, 1990, CA. 2–01
Bristol Corporation v. Persons Unknown [1974] 1 W.L.R. 365; (1973) 118 S.J. 100; [1974] 1 All E.R. 593; (1973) 72 L.G.R. 245. 1–16

Coombes v. Smith [1986] 1 W.L.R. 808; (1986) 130 S.J. 482; [1987] 1 F.L.R. 352; (1987) 17 Fam. Law 123. 1–05
Coventry, dec'd; Re; Coventry v. Coventry [1980] Ch. 461; [1973] 3 W.L.R. 802; (1979) 123 S.J. 606; [1979] 3 All E.R. 815, CA; affirming [1979] 2 W.L.R. 853; (1978) 123 S.J. 406; [1979] 2 All E.R. 408. 2–01

Evers' Trust, Re; Papps v. Evers [1980] 1 W.L.R. 1327; (1980) 124 S.J. 562; [1980] 3 All E.R. 399; (1980) 10 Fam. Law 245, CA. 1–02

G (A Minor) (Parental Responsibility Order), Re [1994] 1 F.L.R. 504; [1994] 2 F.C.R. 1037; [1994] Fam. Law 372, CA. 3–07
Greasley v. Cooke [1980] 1 W.L.R. 1306; (1980) 124 S.J. 629; [1980] 3 All E.R. 710, CA. 1–05, 1–14

H (Illegitimate Children: Fathers: Parental Rights) (No. 2), Re. *See* H (Minors) (Local Authority: Parental Rights) (No. 3), Re
H (Minors) (Local Authority: Parental Rights) (No. 3), Re [1991] Fam. 151; [1991] 2 W.L.R. 763; [1991] 2 All E.R. 185; (1991) 135 S.J. 16; [1991] 1 F.L.R. 214; 89 L.G.R. 537; [1991] Fam. Law 306; [1991] F.C.R. 361; *The Times*, November 21, 1990, CA. 3–07
H v. M (Property: Beneficial Interest) [1992] 1 F.L.R. 229; [1991] Fam. Law 473; [1991] F.C.R. 938; *The Times*, May 2, 1991 1–10
Harwood v. Harwood [1991] 2 F.L.R. 274; [1991] Fam. Law 418; [1992] F.C.R. 1, CA. 1–04

Horner v. Horner [1982] Fam. 90; [1982] 2 W.L.R. 914; [1982] 2
  All E.R. 495; (1982) 12 Fam. Law 144; (1983) 4 F.L.R. 50,
  CA. 4–39
Huntingford v. Hobbs (1992) 24 H.L.R. 652; [1993] 1 F.L.R.
  736; [1992] Fam. Law 437; [1992] N.P.C. 39; [1992]
  E.G.C.S. 38, CA. 1–04

Jessop v. Jessop [1992] 1 F.L.R. 591; [1992] Fam. Law 328;
  [1992] 2 F.C.R. 253; *The Times*, October 16, 1991, CA. ... 2–06
Jones v. Challenger [1961] 1 Q.B. 176; [1960] 2 W.L.R. 695; 104
  S.J. 328; [1960] 1 All E.R. 785; [23 M.L.R. 703; 24 Conv.
  240; 27 Sol. 321; [1960] C.L.J. 167] CA. 1–02

Lloyds Bank v. Rosset [1991] 1 A.C. 107; [1990] 2 W.L.R. 867;
  [1990] 1 All E.R. 1111; [1990] 2 F.L.R. 155; (1990) 22
  H.L.R. 349; (1990) 60 P. & C.R. 311; (1990) 140 N.L.J.
  478, H.L.; reversing [1989] Ch. 350; [1988] 3 W.L.R.
  1301; [1988] 3 All E.R. 915; [1989] 1 F.L.R. 51; [1988]
  Fam. Law 472; [1989] L.S. Gaz. January 5, 39, CA. 1–05

Matharu v. Matharu [1994] 2 F.L.R. 597; [1994] 3 F.C.R. 216;
  (1994) 68 P. & C.R. 93; [1994] Fam. Law 624; [1994]
  E.G.C.S. 87; (1994) 91(25) L.S. Gaz. 31; (1994) 138
  S.J.L.B. 111 [1994] N.P.C. 63; *The Times*, May 13, 1994;
  The Independent, May 18, 1994, CA. 1–05
Midland Bank v. Cooke [1995] 4 All E.R. 562; (1995) 27 H.L.R.
  733; [1995] 2 F.L.R. 915; [1995] Fam. Law 675; [1995]
  N.P.C. 116; (1995) 139 S.J.L.B. 194; (1995) 145 N.L.J.
  Rep. 1543; *The Times*, July 13, 1995; *The Independent*, July
  26, 1995, CA. 1–06

T. v. S (Financial Provision for Children) [1994] 2 F.L.R. 883;
  [1994] 1 F.C.R. 743; [1995] Fam. Law 11, Fam. Div. 1–29
Tanner v. Tanner [1975] 1 W.L.R. 1346; 119 S.J. 391; [1975] 3
  All E.R. 776; 5 Fam. Law 193; *subsequent proceedings, The
  Times*, February 17, 1976, CA. 1–14

Windeler v. Whitehall [1990] 2 F.L.R. 505; (1990) 154 J.P.N. 29;
  [1990] F.C.R. 268. 1–09

TABLE OF STATUTES

1882	Married Women's Property Act (45 & 46 Vict. c. 75)—		1988	Housing Act (c. 50)... 2–07
	s.17 .... 1–10, 1–19			Pt. 1 4–21
1925	Trustee Act (15 & 16 Geo. 5, c. 19)—			s. 17(5) 2–07
				Sched. 4
	s. 41 1–07			para. 2(3) 2–08
	Law of Property Act (15 & 16 Geo, 5, c. 20)—		1989	Children Act (c. 41).. 2–13, 3–26, 3–27, 4–06, 4–24
				s. 1(3) 3–16
	s. 30 .... 1–01, 1–02			s. 2(6) 2–13
1973	Matrimonial Causes Act (c. 18)—			s. 4 3–07
				(3) 2–13
	s. 25 1–05			s. 5(1)(a) 2–13
1975	Inheritance (Provision for Family and Dependants) Act (c. 63)..... 2–01, 2–21			(6) 2–13
				s. 6(7) 2–13
				s. 8 .... 2–13, 2–14, 3–07, 3–16, 3–20
				(2) 2–13
	s. 1A 2–01			s. 9(7) 3–16
	s. 9 2–06			s. 10(4)(a) 2–13
1976	Fatal Accidents Act (c. 30).......... 2–20			s. 11(5) 3–16
				s. 12(1) 3–07
	s. 1(3)(b) 2–20			s. 44A 4–24
	(e) 2–20			Sched. 1 .... 1–10, 1–29, 4–27
	Domestic Violence and Matrimonial Proceedings Act (c. 50)..... 4–01, 4–34			
				para. 1 .... 1–29, 3–33
				para. 2 3–33
				para. 10 3–33
	Rent (Agriculture) Act (c. 80).......... 4–22			para. 11 3–33
			1991	Child Support Act (c. 48)..... 3–02, 3–03, 3–04, 3–05, 3–06, 3–34
1977	Rent Act (c. 42)...... 2–08, 4–21, 4–22			
				s. 27 3–01
	Sched. 1		1995	Law Reform (Succession) Act (c. 41)—
	para. 3 2–08			
1983	Matrimonial Homes Act (c. 19).......... 1–14			s. 2 2–01
			1996	Family Law Act (c. 27)—
	Mental Health Act (c. 20).......... 4–26			
				Pt. II 4–20, 4–22
1985	Housing Act (c. 68)... 4–21			Pt IV .. 4–01, 4–23, 4–24, 4–34, 4–39
1987	Family Law Reform Act (c. 42)..... 3–02, 3–03, 3–04, 3–05, 3–06			
				s. 33 ... 4–03, 4–04, 4–06, 4–31, 4–34
	s. 22 3–01			

1996	Family Law Act—*cont.*		1996	Family Law Act—*cont.*	
	s. 33(2)	4–04, 4–27		s. 47(5)	4–16
	(6)	4–04		(6)	4–17
	(a)	4–06, 4–07, 4–20, 4–27		(7)	4–17
	(b)	4–06, 4–07, 4–20, 4–27, 4–31		(8)	4–18
				(10)	4–18
				s. 48	4–18
				s. 49	4–19
	(c)	4–06, 4–07, 4–20, 4–27, 4–31		s. 53	4–20, 4–27
				s. 59	4–26
				(1)	4–26
	(d)	4–06, 4–07, 4–27, 4–31		s. 62(3)	4–05
				(5)	4–05
	(e)	4–31		s. 63	4–05
	(f)	4–31		Sched. 5	4–18
	(7)	4–04		Sched. 6	4–24
	s. 36	4–06, 4–31		Sched. 7	4–27
	(3)	4–06		Pt. I	4–20
	(4)	4–06		Pt. III	4–22
	(5)	4–06		Sched. 9	
	(6)	4–06		para. 10	4–01
	(e)	4–20, 4–27		Sched. 10	4–01
	(f)	4–20, 4–27		Trusts of Land and Appointment of Trustees Act (c. 47)	1–01
	(g)	4–20, 4–27			
	(h)	4–20, 4–27			
	(i)	4–27			
	(7)	4–06		s. 4	1–02
	(11)	4–06		s. 12	1–02
	s. 38	4–03, 4–07, 4–31		s. 13	1–02
	(4)	4–07		s. 14	1–01, 1–02, 1–07, 1–08, 1–10, 2–12
	s. 39	4–08			
	s. 40	4–32			
	s. 41	4–09, 4–27		s. 15	1–02
	s. 42	4–02, 4–32, 4–34	1997	Protection from Harassment Act (c. 40)	4–39
	s. 43	4–10			
	s. 44	4–11, 4–27		s. 1	4–39, 4–40
	s. 45	4–12, 4–27		s. 3(1)	4–40
	s. 46	4–13		(2)	4–40
	(3)	4–13		(3)	4–40
	s. 47	4–14		(6)	4–40
	(1)	4–14		(7)	4–40
	(2)	4–14		(8)	4–40
	(3)	4–15		(9)	4–40
	(4)	4–16			

TABLE OF STATUTORY INSTRUMENTS

1971	Blood Tests (Evidence of Paternity) Regulations (S.I. 1971 No. 1861).......	3–01	1996	High Court and County Court Jurisdiction (Amendment) Order (S.I. 1996 No. 3141)....... 1–02
	Magistrates Court (Blood Tests) Rules (S.I. 1971 No. 1991).......	3–01	1997	Family Proceedings (Amendment No. 3) Rules (S.I. 1997 No. 1893)....... 4–25
1991	Family Proceedings Rules (S.I. 1991 No. 1247)—			r. 3.9A(6) 4–18
				r. 3.10 4–18
	r. 2.9	3–04		Family Proceedings Courts (Matrimonial Proceedings, etc.) (Amendment) Rules (S.I. 1997 No. 1894)... 4–25
	r. 3.13	3–03		
	r. 3.16	3–03		
	r. 4.14(2)	2–18		
	r. 4.15	2–18		
	r. 4.16	2–18		Family Proceedings Courts (Children Act 1989) (Amendment) Rules (S.I. 1997 No. 1895)... 4–25
	r. 10.2	4–29		
	r. 10.3	4–29		
	Family Proceedings Courts (Children Act 1989) Rules (S.I. 1991 No. 1395)—			
	r. 14(2)	2–18		
	r. 15	2–18		
	r. 16	2–18		

Part I: Actions Relating to Property—Ownership or Occupation

A. Application for an Order for Sale and/or Determination of Beneficial Interests

The Law

Where the legal and beneficial title is held in joint names and the co-owners cannot agree on a sale, then either party can apply under section 14 of the Trusts of Land and Appointment of Trustees Act 1996 for an order that the property be sold and the proceeds of sale be divided in accordance with the respective beneficial interests. If the beneficial interests are not expressly defined in the title documents the court can be asked to determine the extent of those interests. The Trusts of Land and Appointment of Trustees Act (TLATA) 1996 came into force on January 1, 1997 and repeals section 30 of the Law of Property Act 1925. Proceedings already begun under section 30 at that date, continue as proceedings under section 14 of the TLATA.[1]

1–01

The Trusts of Land and Appointment of Trustees Act 1996

Under section 4 of the TLATA 1996 there is to be implied in every trust for sale of land, a power to postpone sale. Section 12 gives a person entitled to a beneficial interest in land the right to occupy the land, and section 13 enables the court to regulate that occupation, but it is likely that most disputes between cohabitants will fall under section 14.

1–02

Under section 14 of the TLATA 1996 the court may make any order:

---

[1] The High Court and County Court Jurisdiction (Amendment) Order 1996 (S.I. 1996 No. 3141).

(a) relating to the exercise by the trustees of any of their functions (including an order relieving them of any obligation to obtain the consent of, or to consult, any person in connection with the exercise of any of their functions); or
(b) declaring the nature or extent of a person's interest in property subject to the trust, as the court thinks fit.

Under section 15 of the TLATA 1996 the matters to which the court must have regard include:

(a) the intention of the person(s) (if any) who created the trust;
(b) the purposes for which the property subject to the trust is held;
(c) the welfare of any minor who occupies or might reasonably be expected to occupy any land subject to the trust as his home; and
(d) the interests of any secured creditor of any beneficiary.

They must have regard to the circumstances and wishes of any beneficiaries of full age and entitled to an interest in possession in property subject to the trust or (in case of dispute) of the majority (according to the value of their combined interests).

The court has discretion to order a sale and will still have to consider whether the underlying purpose for which the property was bought, *e.g.* cohabitation, has come to an end. The case law under section 30 of the Law of Property Act such as *Re Evers Trust*[2] and *Jones v. Challenger*[3] will still be helpful but the court has much wider scope under section 15 and there is an argument for saying that it could make orders more typically found in the matrimonial courts.

The title documents

1–03 Where the beneficial ownership of joint owners is not clearly expressed in the title documents to a property or where a property is in a sole name, one party can apply for a declaration that he or she is entitled to a beneficial interest or greater beneficial interest in the property. The legal title is always held by joint owners as joint tenants. If the beneficial title is not specifically mentioned or is described as a tenancy in common without declaring the shares, there is scope for an application for a declaration of beneficial interests.

---

[2] [1980] 3 All E.R. 399.
[3] [1961] 1 Q.B. 176.

Registered land

If there has been a transfer of registered land to joint owners and the transfer indicates that the survivor can give a valid receipt, that does not necessarily mean that the parties hold as joint tenants.[4] Unless there has been an express declaration that they hold as joint tenants, there will be scope for an application for a declaration of beneficial interests.

1–04

If the transfer indicates that the survivor cannot give a valid receipt, then the parties hold as tenants in common and a restriction will be entered on the register, but, unless there has been an express declaration of their shares, either party can apply for a declaration of beneficial interests.

Implied Trusts

The applicant has to satisfy the court that such an interest has been acquired from a resulting trust, a constructive trust or by proprietory estoppel. The court does not have a discretion to make such order as it thinks fair between the parties as it has under section 25 of the Matrimonial Causes Act 1973. What matters is whether the parties intended to share the beneficial interest.

1–05

The distinction between a resulting trust and a constructive trust was clearly set out in the case of *Lloyds Bank plc v. Rosset.*[5]

A constructive trust arises where there is direct evidence of an agreement, arrangement or understanding between the parties that the beneficial interest in the property was to be shared and the claimant has relied on that to his or her detriment.

A resulting trust arises where the evidence of common intention is inferred from the conduct of the parties and that conduct must amount to the claimant making direct financial contributions to the purchase price.

A claim in proprietory estoppel arises where the claimant can show that he or she has incurred expenditure or otherwise prejudiced him or herself or acted to his or her detriment believing that he or she had an interest in the property or would acquire one and that that belief was encouraged by the owner of the land or someone acting on the owner's behalf.[6] If satisfied, the court can transfer the estate to the claimant, award the claimant a beneficial interest in the property or grant the claimant the right to live in the property.[7]

---

[4] *Harwood v. Harwood* [1991] 2 F.L.R. 274; *Huntingford v. Hobbs* [1993] 1 F.L.R. 736.
[5] [1990] 1 All E.R. 1111.
[6] *Matharu v. Matharu* [1994] 2 F.L.R. 597.
[7] *Greasley v. Cooke* [1980] 1 W.L.R. 1306; *Coombes v. Smith* [1986] 1 W.L.R. 808.

Quantifying the shares

1–06 If there has been an express agreement about the size of the shares, that will be conclusive. If not, the court will quantify the contributions made by each party taking into account all conduct. This would appear to include home making and child rearing.[8]

Protective measures

1–07 Where the title is held in one sole name and the other party can establish that he or she has a beneficial interest, *e.g.* based on the doctrine of resulting or constructive trusts, he or she should protect his or her rights by seeking appointment as a second trustee.[9] If he or she has been appointed second trustee and refuses to join in a sale, then the legal owner would have to apply for a section 14 TLATA order. If he or she has not been appointed and the legal owner refuses to sell, he or she can apply for a section 14 order.

If the land is registered and the claimant is not in occupation, then a restriction, notice or caution should be registered and the interest then becomes a protected minor interest binding on any purchaser or mortgagee. The claimant would then have notice of any attempted disposal or dealing with the land and could seek an injunction to prevent the transaction from going through. This is easier to achieve once a beneficial interest has been established. If the claimant is in occupation, the beneficial interest may be an overriding interest.

If the land is not registered, the interest should not strictly be registered as a land charge. However, it is probably a sensible precaution, even if it has to be cleared from the register later, because by that time the purchaser or mortgagee should have notice. If proceedings have already begun, then a pending land action can be registered.

If in doubt about the appropriate form of relief, refer to the checklist in Appendix 2 and the flowchart in Appendix 3.

THE PROCEDURE

Court

1–08 Section 14 TLATA proceedings can be started in the High Court or the county court. High Court proceedings are usually started in the Chancery Division but it has been said that cases involving

---

[8] *Midland Bank v. Cooke* and another [1995] 2 F.L.R. 915.
[9] Trustee Act 1925, s. 41.

couples living together could be started in the Family Division or transferred to it.[10] The county court has unlimited jurisdiction and proceedings should be started in the court for the district in which the respondent lives or carries on business or where the property is situated.

Pleadings

Proceedings are begun by originating summons in the High Court or originating application in the county court, supported by affidavit, setting out the terms of the order sought, the grounds in support, the name and address of the person to be served and the applicant's address for service.[11] If there appears to be a substantial conflict of evidence or if the plaintiff's claim is based on an allegation of fraud, a writ of summons is appropriate.

In the High Court, the plaintiff files the originating summons and, where appropriate, notice of issue of legal aid. The summons is issued and returned to the plaintiff for service. Within one month of the expiry of the time within which copies of affidavit evidence may be served under Order 28, rule 1A (see Service, below) the plaintiff must obtain an appointment before the court which is fixed by notice in Form 12.

In the county court, the applicant files the originating application with copies for the Respondent(s) and a request for issue and, where appropriate, notice of issue of legal aid. The proper officer of the court then fixes a return day, prepares notice to each party, annexes a copy to each copy of the application and delivers a plaint note to the applicant. The return day is the day fixed for the hearing or for a pre-trial review.

The respondent can file and serve an affidavit in reply. The affidavits should deal with matters relevant to the order or directions sought, *e.g.* to show that the purpose of the trust for sale has come to an end, that a sale is necessary, that it is advisable to sell in the way proposed or why conduct of the sale should be given to a particular person. If a declaration of beneficial interests is sought, the affidavits should set out the details supporting the contention that a constructive or resulting trust exists and/or justifying the shares sought.

If the case is based on a constructive or resulting trust, the originating summons or statement of claim will usually seek a declaration that the property is held by the defendant/respondent and the plaintiff/applicant as beneficial joint tenants or tenants in common in specific shares. Alternatively, the plaintiff/applicant can

1–09

---

[10] *Bernard v. Josephs* [1982] Ch. 391.
[11] RSC, Ord. 7 and CCR, Ord. 3, r. 4.

ask the court to determine his or her beneficial interest in the property.

If the case is based on proprietory estoppel, the plaintiff/applicant will seek a declaration that he or she is entitled to the interest sought and an order that the defendant/respondent grant the relevant interest to the plaintiff/applicant. The particulars of the assurances or representations made by the defendant/respondent on which the plaintiff/applicant relied should be set out in the affidavit or statement of claim. A claim in proprietory estoppel may be pleaded as an alternative to a claim based on a constructive or resulting trust. The court is unlikely to apply this doctrine if it is not pleaded: see *Windeler v. Whitehall*.[12]

H v. M[13] guidelines

1–10   (1) All possible issues should be raised at the earliest stage "so that an informed judgment can be made as to the forum and procedure providing the quickest and most cost effective outcome". If separate proceedings have been started relating to, *e.g.* partnership assets or Schedule 1 to the Children Act as well as section 14 of the TLATA, it would seem sensible to seek to consolidate them at the first directions appointment.
(2) If ownership of personal property is disputed, the proper action is for a declaration or inquiry as to the beneficial interest, supported by affidavit evidence on lines similar to the procedure for resolving disputes under section 17 of the Married Women's Property Act 1882.
(3) Discovery orders should be made early and enforced strictly.
(4) Claims to beneficial interests in substantial assets should be supported by detailed pleading as to any express discussions between the parties, however imperfectly remembered. "The tenderest exchanges of a common law courtship may assume an unforeseen significance many years later when they are brought under equity's microscope."

Service

1–11 The originating summons in the High Court must be served personally on the defendant or a copy sent by first class post or by inserting through the letter box of the defendant's last known

---
[12] [1990] 2 F.L.R. 505.
[13] [1992] 1 F.L.R. 229.

address unless the defendant's solicitor endorses on the summons that he accepts service. The affidavit in support must be served within 14 days of the defendant acknowledging service. The defendant should file his affidavit in response within 28 days.[14] Notice of the appointment for the first hearing should be served at least 14 days beforehand.[15]

An originating application in the county court may be served by delivering it to the respondent personally, or as is more usual, by an officer of the court sending it by first class post to the respondent. In the latter case, service is deemed to be the seventh day after the date on which the application was sent.[16] Service must be effected not less than 21 days before the return day but, without prejudice to the power to abridge time for service,[17] service may be effected at any time if the court is satisfied, on affidavit evidence, that the respondent is about to move.

Directions

Directions can be given for filing of (further) affidavits, Scott Schedules, discovery and inspection, valuation, expert evidence, where appropriate accounts and inquiries, and setting down.[18] The court may direct notice of the action (in proper form) be served on any person who is not a party but who will or may be affected by any judgment. The notice must be accompanied by a copy of the pleadings and the prescribed form of acknowledgment of service.

1–12

Order

The court may make a declaration as to the plaintiff's beneficial interest in the property; or make a declaration that the property is held by the plaintiff and the defendant as beneficial joint tenants or tenants in common in specific shares; or make an order that the defendant grant the plaintiff the relevant interest in the property under proprietary estoppel. The court may also make an order for sale of the property and for distribution of the net sale proceeds. Equitable accounting may be necessary for, *e.g.* apportioning sale proceeds to take account of money spent on the property after separation which preserves or enhances the value of it or giving credit to a person left in possession pending sale or transfer for the capital element of the mortgage instalments paid on behalf of the other party.

1–13

---

[14] RSC, Ord. 28, r. 1A.
[15] RSC, Ord. 28, r. 3.
[16] CCR, Ord. 7,r. 10(3).
[17] CCR, Ord. 13, r. 4.
[18] RSC, Ord. 25 and 28, r. 4.

The court can give further directions, at the same time as an order for sale or afterwards, dealing with some or all of following:

- necessary accounts and inquiries;
- appointing person who is to have conduct of the sale;
- fixing manner of sale, *e.g.* private treaty, public auction reserve or minimum price;
- giving leave to bid at auction;
- requiring payment of purchase money into court or to trustees or other persons where necessary, directing that incumbrances be paid off or that an amount, sufficient to cover the incumbrance and any interest due on it and perhaps also an additional amount to cover any contingencies, be paid into court;
- settling particulars and conditions of sale;
- fixing remuneration of auctioneer, where appropriate;
- investigation of title or settling of conveyance by conveyancing counsel.

The tendency is to keep such directions to a minimum and to leave such matters to the discretion of the person with conduct of the sale. Where the defendant has defaulted and can be shown to be likely to continue to default, a direction can be given that all documents necessary to effect a sale be executed by a district judge or Master.

Conduct of the sale is normally given to the plaintiff or plaintiff's solicitors or the solicitors for the party who has the deeds, but not normally to a person who has leave to bid as a prospective purchaser. The party who has the deeds must co-operate and any interference may be restrained by injunction. The solicitor of the party who has conduct of the sale is the agent of all the parties to the action as between vendor and purchaser.

In general, a declaration is made by a judge in open court and an inquiry is conducted by a Master or district judge.

If a judgment affects rights or interests or persons not parties to the action, the court may direct notice of the judgment be given in proper form.

The Precedents

A1. Originating Summons for Order for Sale and/or Declaration of Beneficial Interests

IN THE HIGH COURT OF JUSTICE   No.
CHANCERY/FAMILY DIVISION
    DISTRICT REGISTRY

IN THE MATTER OF *[Address of property and registered title number]*
AND IN THE MATTER OF THE TRUSTS OF LAND AND APPOINTMENT OF TRUSTEES ACT 1996, s. 14

BETWEEN

                                        Plaintiff

                  and

                                        Defendant

To *[Defendant's name]* of *[address]*

Let the Defendant within 14 days after service of this summons on him, counting the day of service, return the accompanying Acknowledgment of Service to the appropriate court office.

By this summons, which is issued on the application of the Plaintiff *[name]* of *[address]*, the Plaintiff claims the following relief:-

(1) a Declaration that the Plaintiff and the Defendant hold the property known as *[describe property]* as beneficial joint tenants or as tenants in common (in equal shares) (as to the Plaintiff *[number]* per cent and as to the Defendant *[number]* per cent) (in such shares as the court thinks fit)

(2) an order for the sale of the freehold property known as *[describe property]* by *[auction or as the case may be describing the mode of sale proposed]*

(3) an order that the proceeds of sale be (lodged in court to the credit of this action) (paid to the trustees for the time being of *[describe the trust instrument]*) (divided between the Plaintiff and the Defendant in accordance with their beneficial shares or as the case may be)

(4) such consequential directions as may be necessary *[For alternative directions, see under "Order" at 1–13 above]*

(5) that provision be made for the costs of this application

If the Defendant does not acknowledge service, such judgment may be given or order made against or in relation to him as the court may think just and expedient.

DATED the   day of

Note — This summons may not be served later than 4 calendar months (or if leave is required to effect service out of the jurisdiction 6 months) beginning with the above date unless renewed by order of the court.

This summons was taken out by   of
(Agents for)   of   Solicitors for the Plaintiff

IMPORTANT
Directions for the Acknowledgment of Service are given with the accompanying form

A2. Originating Application for Order for Sale and/or Declaration of Beneficial Interests

IN THE   COUNTY COURT   No.

IN THE MATTER OF *[Address of property and registered title number]*

AND IN THE MATTER OF THE TRUSTS OF LAND AND APPOINTMENT OF TRUSTEES ACT 1996, s.14

BETWEEN:

Applicant

and

Respondent

[Name] of *[address]* applies to the court for the following:

(1) a Declaration that the Applicant and the Respondent hold the property known as *[describe property]* as beneficial joint tenants or as tenants in common (in equal shares) (as to the Applicant *[number]* per cent and as to the Respondent *[number]* per cent) (in such shares as the court thinks fit)

(2) an Order for the sale of the freehold property known as *[describe property]* by *[auction or as the case may be describing the mode of sale proposed]*

(3) an order that the proceeds of sale be (lodged in court to the credit of this action) (paid to the trustees for the time being of *[describe the trust instrument]*) (divided between the Applicant and the Respondent in accordance with their beneficial shares or as the case may be)

(4) such consequential directions as may be necessary *[For alternative directions, see under "Order" at 1–13 above]*

(5) that provision be made for the costs of this application.

The grounds on which I claim to be entitled to the Order are set out in the accompanying affidavit.

The name and address of the person upon whom it is intended to serve this application is *[name]* of *[address]*

My address for service is *[address]*

DATED this   day of

....

Applicant or Solicitors for the Applicant

A3. Affidavit in Support of Originating Summons or Originating Application for Order for Sale

(Plaintiff/Applicant)
[name]
1st
[date]

[High Court or county court heading as A1 or A2 above]

I *[name]* of *[address and occupation or description]* make oath and say as follows:-

1. I am the (Plaintiff/Applicant) herein and I make this affidavit in support of my application for an order for the sale of the property known as *[describe the property]*.

2. By a transfer dated the   day of   made between *[name]* and *[name]* of the one part and the (Defendant/Respondent) and me of the other part the said property was transferred to the (Defendant/Respondent) and me as tenants in common. The transfer indicated that the survivor could not give a valid receipt and a restriction was entered on registration of the title under Title number *[number]*.

By a declaration of trust dated the same date as the said transfer and made between me of the one part and the (Defendant/Respondent) of the other part we agreed and declared that we held the beneficial title to the said property as to sixty per cent to me and as to forty per cent to the (Defendant/Respondent).

3. The said property was purchased for the (Defendant/Respondent) and me to live in as our home together.

4. I left the (Defendant/Respondent) on the   day of   and we have not lived together since. The purpose of the trust has therefore come to an end and I wish to realise my interest in the said property either by selling it and dividing the net proceeds of sale in accordance with the declaration of trust or by transferring it to the (Defendant/Respondent) in consideration of a sum equivalent to sixty per cent of the equity. I have asked the (Defendant/Respondent) on numerous occasions to sell or purchase my interest and she refuses to give me an answer.

5. I therefore humbly beseech this Honourable Court to order the sale of the said property by private treaty.

SWORN at
in the County of
this   day of

BEFORE ME

14 ACTIONS RELATING TO PROPERTY—OWNERSHIP OR OCCUPATION

A4. Affidavit in Reply to Originating Summons or Originating Application For Order For Sale

(Defendant/Respondent)
[name]
1st
[date]

[High Court or county court heading as A1 or A2 above]

I *[name]* of *[address and occupation or description]* make oath and say as follows:-

1. I am the (Defendant/Respondent) herein and I make this affidavit in response to the (Plaintiff's/Applicant's) application for an order for sale of the property known as *[describe property]* and affidavit in support sworn the   day of   .

2. I refer to the (Plaintiff's/Applicant's) said affidavit and paragraphs 2 and 3 are correct.

3. We lived together in the said property as husband and wife and on the   day of
I gave birth to twin boys namely *[name]* and *[name]*. The (Plaintiff/Applicant) is the father. We planned to have children from the outset and it was always intended that the property should be the family home.

4. On the   day of   a huge argument developed between us during which the (Plaintiff/Applicant) said that he had discovered that I had been carrying on with someone else and that the twins were not his. I vehemently denied this but he would not listen and became extremely violent hitting me repeatedly about the face and body. I called the police who took him away and on the   day of   I was granted an occupation order and non-molestation order by the *[name]* County Court No. *[case number]*. We have not lived together since.

5. I oppose the application for an order for sale on the basis that the purpose of the trust for sale has not come to an end as the property is still providing a home for me and the children and will continue to do so until the children are grown up. I therefore humbly beseech this Honourable Court to dismiss the application.

SWORN AT
in the County of
this   day of
BEFORE ME

A5. Affidavit Supporting Originating Summons or Originating Application for Declaration as to Beneficial Ownership and Order for Sale

Plaintiff
[name]
1st
[date]

[High Court or County Court heading as A1 or A2 above]

BETWEEN

Plaintiff/Applicant

and

Defendant/Respondent

I, *[Name]* of *[address and occupation and description]* make oath and say as follows:-

1. I am the (Plaintiff/Applicant) herein and I make this affidavit in support of my claim for a beneficial interest in *[describe property]* and for an order for sale of the said property in order to realise my share.

2. I met the (Defendant/Respondent) in about May *[year]* and by August *[year]* we were living together as husband and wife at *[address]* which was a property owned by the (Defendant/Respondent) in his sole name. I was still married to someone else at the time and the (Defendant/Respondent) said that he would not put the property in joint names as my husband might have some claim on it. I took legal advice to the effect that this was a possibility and so I accepted the situation. However I believed that this was the only reason he did not put the property in joint names and that in any other situation he would have done. I believed that he wanted me to have an interest in the property.

3. My decree absolute came through in November *[year]* and all financial matters between me and my former husband were settled at that time. I did not mention putting the property in joint names then or at all because I felt comfortable that the (Defendant/Respondent) intended me to have an interest in it. He always referred to it as our house.

4. From September *[year]* until we separated in January *[year]* I contributed to the mortgage and the household expenses because

my salary was paid into a joint account with the *[name of bank]* Bank of *[address]* account number *[number]* which I held jointly with the (Defendant/Respondent). I never saw the bank statements because the (Defendant/Respondent) took care of all financial matters but I believe that the mortgage was paid from that account. I believe that the mortgage was with the *[name]* Building Society because I occasionally saw letters arrive for the (Defendant/Respondent) from them.

5. I was working throughout the time I was living with the (Defendant/Respondent) as a secretary earning between £*[amount]* and £*[amount]* per month net. The (Defendant/Respondent) was a self-employed computer consultant and I never had any idea how much he earned. He had only started the business just before we met and he was always moaning that he did not earn much.

6. During the time I lived at *[address]* I redecorated the living room, dining room and two bedrooms. We bought a new three piece suite, dining table and chairs, freezer, microwave and complete bedroom suite for the main bedroom and many other smaller items from the joint bank account.

7. We separated on the *[date]* and since then I have claimed a share of the property and have asked the (Defendant/Respondent) to sell so that I can have a share of the proceeds of sale. He refuses to accept that I am entitled to a share and refuses to sell.

8. I humbly beseech this Honourable Court to declare that the property is held by the (Defendant/Respondent) and me as beneficial tenants in common in equal shares or such shares as the court deems fit as a result of a resulting trust or constructive trust or proprietory estoppel. I also seek an order for sale so that I can realise my share in the property and I believe that an order should be made that I have conduct of the sale as I do not believe that the (Defendant/Respondent) would co-operate.

SWORN AT
in the County of
this   day of

BEFORE ME

A6. Affidavit in Reply to Originating Summons or Originating Application for Declaration as to Beneficial Ownership and Order for Sale

(Defendant/Respondent)
[name]
1st
[date]

[High Court or county court heading as A1 or A2 above]

I *[name]* of *[address and occupation or description]* make oath and say as follows:-

1. I am the (Defendant/Respondent) herein and I make this affidavit in reply to the application for a declaration as to beneficial ownership and for an order for sale.

2. I refer to the (Plaintiff's/Applicant's) affidavit sworn on the day of

3. It is true that I met the (Plaintiff/Applicant) in about May *[year]*. At that time she was still living with her husband. I lived in my own house which I had purchased in my sole name in *[year]*. I paid £60,000 for it in *[year]* by paying a deposit of £20,000 and taking out a mortgage for £40,000 with the *[name]* Building Society.

4. In August *[year]* the (Plaintiff/Applicant) was having a very bad time at home with her husband and was desperate to find somewhere else to live. I offered to let her come and stay with me on a short term basis. I most definitely did not say anything to her about putting my property into joint names. If it had been mentioned I would not have agreed to it. We had only known each other about three months. By that time my property was worth about £200,000 and I would never have agreed to hand over one half of that to someone I barely knew. My agreement to let her stay was an act of compassion only. I did express concern at the time about whether living with me would affect her divorce proceedings but I did not mean by that that I would not put the property into joint names because her husband might have some claim. The (Plaintiff/Applicant) has made all that up.

5. Our relationship did develop and we continued to live together as husband and wife until January *[year]*. The question of ownership of the property was never mentioned. If I did ever refer to the property as our house I meant that it was our home, not that we shared ownership of it.

6. We did open a joint account with the *[name]* Bank and the (Plaintiff's/Applicant's) salary was paid into it. However she withdrew one half of her salary each month. I believe that she paid this into a Building Society account in her sole name and I put her to proof of all savings and investments in her name. The remainder of her salary barely covered her half share of the food and household bills and made no contribution whatsoever towards the mortgage. She simply paid for her keep and no more.

7. I always paid the mortgage. The mortgage payments were not particularly high and I was always able to make them even during the early days of my self employment. It did take a few months to build up my business but by the time the (Plaintiff/Applicant) came to live with me I was doing quite well. I sometimes moaned that clients were slow to pay my invoices but I earned a reasonably good living. The (Plaintiff/Applicant) did not contribute to the mortgage in any way.

8. The (Plaintiff/Applicant) did do some decorating but I do not believe that this entitles her to share in my house. We did buy certain items from the joint account but as the (Plaintiff's/Applicant's) contribution to that account only covered her share of the living expenses I do not accept that she contributed to the purchase of those items and I believe that they are mine.

9. I ask this court to dismiss the (Plaintiff's/Applicant's) claim for a beneficial share in my property and thus dismiss her claim for an order for sale.

SWORN AT
in the County of
this   day of

BEFORE ME

A7. Notice to Person Not a Party who will or may be affected by any Judgment

To be used on applications for an order for sale or applications for declaration of beneficial ownership where third party interests may be affected

[Heading as A1 above]

To: *[name]* and *[address]*

TAKE NOTICE THAT:

(1) An action has been begun in the High Court of Justice in accordance with the Writ of Summons or Originating Summons attached hereto;

(2) you (are or may be one of) the person(s) who (is or are) interested in the (estate or trust property) to which the action relates;

(3) you may within 14 days after service of this notice acknowledge service of the (Writ or Originating Summons) by properly completing the attached acknowledgment of service and (handing it in at or sending it by post to) (Chancery Chambers, Royal Courts of Justice, Strand, London WC2A 2LL or District Registry (address)) and thereby become a party to the action.

(4) If you do not acknowledge service of the (Writ or Originating Summons) you will be bound by any judgment given in the action as if you were a party to it

DATED

A8. Notice of Appointment to Hear Originating Summons

[Heading as in A1 above]

To *[Defendant's name]* of *[address]*

TAKE NOTICE THAT:

(a) The originating summons issued herein on the   day of   will be heard by the Judge/ Master/ District Judge at Room No. Royal Courts of Justice, Strand, London WC2A 2LL / the District Registry of the High Court of Justice at
on   day the   day of   at   o'clock

(b) At the hearing *[Plaintiff's name]* will seek an (order in the terms of paragraphs 1 to 4 of the originating summons) (the following directions or orders:-

)

(c) You may attend in person or by your solicitor or Counsel. If you fail to attend or to be represented, the court may proceed in your absence.

Dated the   day of

Signed ....

(Agent for) Solicitor for the Plaintiff

A9. Order Declaring Beneficial Ownership and Ordering Sale

[High Court or county court heading as A1 or A2 above]
[Mr. Justice   ]
[Master   or District Judge   ]
[day the   day of   ]

UPON THE APPLICATION of the Plaintiff/Applicant by (Originating Summons/Originating Application) dated *[date]*

AND UPON HEARING [Counsel or the Solicitors] for the Plaintiff/Applicant and for the Defendant/Respondent

AND UPON READING (the documents recorded in the Court file as having been read)

IT IS DECLARED that the (Plaintiff and the Defendant) (the Applicant and the Respondent) hold the freehold property known as *[describe property]* (as beneficial joint tenants) (as tenants in common in (equal shares) (the following shares that is to say as to *[number]* per cent to the Plaintiff/Applicant and as to *[number]* per cent to the Defendant/Respondent))

AND IT IS ORDERED that the said property be sold with vacant possession (by private treaty at a price not less than £ *[number]*) (by public auction and the (Plaintiff and the Defendant) (the Applicant and the Respondent) are to be at liberty to bid at such a sale and to become the purchaser of the said property and the reserve price and remuneration of the auctioneer be fixed by the court in default of agreement) (as the parties may agree or in default of agreement as shall be directed by the court)

AND THIS COURT HEREBY APPOINTS *[name and address]* pursuant to section 50 of the Trustee Act 1925 to convey the said freehold property

AND IT IS ORDERED that the conduct of the sale be given to *[name and address]*

AND IT IS ORDERED that in default of agreement the net proceeds of sale after payment of (the amount outstanding on a mortgage dated *[date]* and made between *[name]* and *[name]* and) the estate agents/auctioneers charges and solicitors conveyancing costs be lodged in court to the credit of this action

[If a summary order for sale has been made at an early stage of the proceedings:

AND IT IS ORDERED that the following inquiry be made that is to say an inquiry as to what estates and interests and in what shares and proportions the Plaintiff and Defendant respectively are interested in the said freehold property or the net proceeds of sale thereof taking into account the mutual dealings of the parties] OR

AND IT IS ORDERED that the net proceeds of sale be divided between the Plaintiff and the Defendant *OR* the Applicant and the Respondent in accordance with their beneficial shares

AND IT IS ORDERED that the Plaintiff's costs of this action be taxed if not agreed and charged against the Defendant's share of the proceeds of sale

AND there be liberty to apply

DATED the   day of

A10. Notice of Judgment to Person Not a Party who may be affected by it

To be used when an order for sale or an order declaring beneficial ownership has been made

[Heading as A1 above]

TAKE NOTICE that a (Judgment or Order) of this Court was (given or made on the   day of

(by which it was *[state substance of judgment or order]*) (a copy of which is attached)

AND ALSO TAKE NOTICE that from the time of service of this Notice you will be bound by the said (Judgment or Order) to the same extent you would have been if you had originally been made a party

AND ALSO TAKE NOTICE that you may within one month after service of this notice apply to the Court to discharge vary or add to the said (Judgment or Order) and that after acknowledging service of this notice you may attend the proceedings under the said (Judgment or Order)

DATED

To: *[name]*

A11. Summons For Declaration as to Beneficial Interest in Deposit Account or in Contents and Order for Sale

[High Court or county court heading as A1 or A2 above]

To *[Defendant's name]* of *[address]*

Let the Defendant within 14 days after service of this summons on him, counting the day of service, return the accompanying Acknowledgment of Service to the appropriate Court Office

By this summons, which is issued on the application of the Plaintiff *[Plaintiff's name]* of *[address]* the Plaintiff claims the following relief, namely:

(1) a Declaration that the deposit account number *[account number]* with the *[name]* Bank is held by the Plaintiff and the Defendant as beneficial joint tenants or as tenants in common in equal shares

(2) alternatively, a declaration or alternatively, an Inquiry, as to the beneficial interest of the Plaintiff in the said deposit account

(3) an Order declaring that (*[list specific items]*) (the items listed in the Schedule hereto) (the contents of the dwelling house and premises known as *[address]*) are the joint property of the Plaintiff and the Defendant and should be divided between them as the court thinks fit

(4) an Order that the said items/contents be sold by (the Plaintiff through his agents *[name]* of *[address]* at a price which the said agents advise is the best price reasonably obtainable in the circumstances)(public auction without reserve prices being fixed)

(5) that directions be given for (preparing particulars of the said contents or a catalogue or fixing the remuneration of the agent or auctioneer)

(6) that in default of agreement the proceeds of sale after deduction of the costs of sale be lodged in court to the credit of this action

(7) that provision be made for the costs of this application

If the Defendant does not acknowledge service, such judgment may be given or order made against or in relation to him as the court may think just and expedient

DATED the   day of

Note - This summons may not be served later than 4 calendar months (or if leave is required to effect service out of the jurisdiction 6 months) beginning with the above date unless renewed by order of the court

B. Possession Proceedings

The Law

1–14 A cohabitant has no right of occupation under the Matrimonial Homes Act 1983 and so if he or she does not have a beneficial interest, he or she will only be able to establish a right to live in the home if he or she has a licence to do so. The most common arrangement for cohabitants is a bare licence, *i.e.* gratuitous permission to occupy which can be revoked at any time without liability upon giving reasonable notice to quit. In certain circumstances where it can be shown that there was an intention to create legal relations and consideration has been given[19], a contractual licence may be established. Such a licence can only be revoked in accordance with the terms of the contract and the licensor is liable in damages if the revocation was in breach of those terms. The court may impose an equitable licence, where a legal owner had induced a claimant to believe that he or she has a right to occupy the home and has acted to his or her detriment relying on that assurance[20], or may find that there is a licence by estoppel where the legal owner is estopped from denying the claimant's right of occupation.

Reasonable notice to quit must be given and what is reasonable depends on the circumstances of the case and whether there are children. At least a month's notice should be given.

Once the licence has been terminated, a licensee who remains in occupation becomes a trespasser and the owner may seek a possession order.

The Procedure

Court

1–15 Possession proceedings can be started in the Chancery Division or Queen's Bench Division of the High Court or in the county court.

Pleadings

1–16 A summary order for possession may be made against a person who has entered into occupation with the consent of the person entitled to possession but remains in occupation without such

---

[19] *Tanner v. Tanner* [1975] 3 All E.R. 737.
[20] *Greasley v. Cooke* [1980] 1 W.L.R. 1306.

consent or licence.[21] This procedure is more appropriate for the eviction of squatters so should not be used if there is the slightest doubt about the claim. Proceedings are begun by writ or originating summons in the High Court or by fixed date action in the county court. The statement or particulars of claim should set out the plaintiff owner's proprietary interest, the licence under which the defendant sharer went into occupation and the facts establishing the plaintiff's claim to possession. If opposed, the defendant should file a defence setting out the grounds for opposing the claim within 14 days of service.[22] Except in a case of urgency and by leave of the court, the day fixed for hearing is not less than five days after the day of service in the case of residential premises and not less than two days after service in the case of other land.

Service

The rules as to service which apply are the same as those for an originating summons or application—see section A above. **1–17**

Order

Provided the court is satisfied as to the plaintiff's claim, it will **1–18** make an order for possession on such terms as it thinks fit. Where the original entry was unlawful, possession must be forthwith, but where it was lawful, Order 24, rule 5(4) enables the court to postpone. If, at the hearing, a triable issue arises, the court can determine it. The judge has a discretion to decide whether summary proceedings should continue or whether the matter should be adjourned for a further hearing after the parties have had time to consider the issues raised.

A warrant to enforce an order may be issued at any time after the making of an order but not more than three months after the date of the order and not before the date for possession.

---

[21] *Bristol Corporation v. persons unknown* [1974] 1 All E.R. 593.
[22] CCR, Ord. 9.

The Precedents

B1. Summons for Possession

IN THE HIGH COURT OF JUSTICE   No.
   DIVISION
   DISTRICT REGISTRY

BETWEEN:

Plaintiff

and

Defendant

STATEMENT OF CLAIM

1. The Plaintiff is and was at all material times the (owner) (tenant) in possession of land and premises known as *[address]*

2. (On or about the *[date]* the Plaintiff orally granted the Defendant a licence to occupy the said land and premises with him/her) (By an agreement in writing dated *[date]* and made between the Plaintiff and the Defendant the Plaintiff granted the Defendant a licence to occupy the said land and premises with him/her) and (the Defendant gave no consideration therefor) (the Defendant gave consideration for the said licence in that he/she *[give details of the consideration given]*.

3. (It was an implied term of the said licence that the same should be terminable on reasonable notice and one month constitutes reasonable notice) (It was an express term of the said licence that the same would be terminable on one month's notice)

4. On the *[date]* the Plaintiff wrote to the Defendant terminating the said licence as from the *[date]*

5. The Defendant wrongfully remains in occupation of the said land and premises as a trespasser

AND the Plaintiff claims:

(1) A declaration that the Defendant's right to occupy *[address]* has been determined

(2) Possession of the said land and premises

(3) An injunction to restrain the Defendant by him/herself, his/her servants or agents or otherwise from occupying the said land and premises

(4) Damages for trespass

(5) Costs

Served the   day of   by   of
Solicitors for the above named Plaintiff.

B2. County Court Claim for Possession

IN THE   COUNTY COURT   No.
BETWEEN:

Plaintiff

and

Defendant

[Name] of *[address and occupation]* hereby applies to the court for an order for recovery of possession of *[describe property]* on the ground that s/he is entitled to possession and that the person in occupation of the premises is in occupation without licence or consent

The person in occupation who is intended to be served with this application is *[name and address of Defendant]*

(There are other persons in occupation whose names are not known to the Plaintiff)

The Plaintiff's address for service is *[address]*

Dated this   day of

B3. Originating Summons For Declaration by Licencee that his/her Licence has not been Terminated

[Heading as B1 above]

TO *[Defendant]* of *[address]*

LET the Defendant within 14 days after service of this summons on him/her counting the day of service return the accompanying Acknowledgment of Service to the appropriate court office

By this summons which is issued on the application of the Plaintiff *[name]* of *[address]* the Plaintiff claims against the Defendant:

(1) A declaration that a licence in writing dated the *[date]* whereby the Defendant granted to the Plaintiff the right to occupy the land and premises known as *[address]* is not revocable by the Defendant except in breach by the Plaintiff of the terms of the said licence

(2) Alternatively, a declaration that the said licence is valid and effective until after the expiration of a reasonable notice period and that the said period is 12 months or such other period as this Honourable Court thinks fit

(3) *[Such other relief as may be appropriate, e.g. an injunction restraining the Defendant from revoking the licence or damages for revocation in breach]*

If the Defendant does not acknowledge service, such judgment may be given or order made against or in relation to him/her as the Court may think fit

DATED the   day of

NOTE - This Summons may not be served later than 4 (or if leave is required to effect service out of the jurisdiction 6) calendar months beginning with the above date unless renewed by order of the Court

This summons was taken out by   of
Solicitors for the said Plaintiff whose address is as stated above.

IMPORTANT
Directions for Acknowledgment of Service are given with the accompanying form

B4. Defence By Licensee Denying Termination of Licence

[Heading as B1 above]

DEFENCE

1. Paragraph 1 of the Statement of Claim is admitted

2. Paragraphs 2 and 3 of the Statement of Claim are admitted save that an implied term of the agreement was that the Defendant should be allowed to occupy the said land and premises until the youngest child of the relationship between the Plaintiff and the Defendant attained the age of 17 years or ceased full time education whichever should be the later. Furthermore the Defendant gave consideration for that agreement by giving up a secure tenancy in her sole name to occupy the premises with the Plaintiff.

3. The Defendant admits receipt of the letter mentioned in paragraph 4 of the Statement of Claim but avers that the Plaintiff's purported revocation of the licence is in breach of the agreement.

4. The Defendant admits that she has occupied and continues to occupy the said premises. She is caring for two children of the relationship namely *[name]* born on *[date of birth]* and *[name]* born on *[date of birth]* who occupy the said premises with her and she requires the said accommodation for them until the youngest child attains the age of 17 years or ceases full time education whichever shall be the later. By virtue of the agreement aforesaid the Defendant was and is entitled to remain in occupation.

Served the   day of
by   of   Solicitors for the Defendant.

B5. Order For Possession

In the *[name]* County Court

Case no.

App. ref.

Applicant

Respondent

On hearing

(and on reading the affidavit(s) of   )

IT IS ORDERED that the applicant do recover possession of the land mentioned in the originating application in this matter namely *[describe land]*

(Where Respondent named and court exercises its jurisdiction to postpone)

AND IT IS ORDERED that the Respondent do give possession of the said land on the *[date]*

AND THAT the applicant do recover against the respondent the sum of £   for costs (or his costs of this action to be taxed on Scale   )

AND FURTHER THAT the respondent do pay the applicant the sum mentioned above by *[date]*

(or do pay the amount of costs when taxed by that day or, if the costs have not been taxed, within 14 days of taxation)

TAKE NOTICE

To the Respondent

If you were occupying these premises when an interim possession order was served and you return as a trespasser within one year of that date you may be arrested and on conviction sent to prison and/or fined (Criminal Justice and Public Order Act 1994, section 76). If you do not pay the costs when they are due and the applicant takes steps to enforce payment, the order will be registered in the Register of County Court Judgments. This may make it difficult for you to get credit. Further information about registration is available in a leaflet which you can get from any county court office

Address for payment

How to Pay

PAYMENTS MUST BE MADE to the person named at the address for payment quoting their reference and the court case number

DO NOT bring or send payments to the court. THEY WILL NOT BE ACCEPTED

You should allow at least 4 days for your payment to reach the applicant or his representative

Make sure that you keep records and can account for all payments made. Proof may be required if there is any disagreement. It is not safe to send cash unless you use registered post

A leaflet giving further advice about payment can be obtained from the court

If you need further information you should contact the applicant or his representative

The court office at
is open from 10.00 a.m. to 4.00 p.m. Mon. to Fri.

C. Application Under Section 17 of the Married Women's Property Act 1882

THE LAW

A fiancé or fiancée can apply for a declaration or enforcement of proprietory rights in property which they possessed or controlled at the time of the application. Property includes the home, contents, dowry, wedding presents and partnership disputes. A person can also apply where they claim that the respondent has had in his possession or control money or property in which the applicant had a beneficial share or interest and that either the money or property has ceased to be in that person's possession or control or the applicant does not know.

1–19

THE PROCEDURE

Court

The High Court and county court have equal jurisdiction. County court proceedings must be begun in the court for the district in which the applicant or respondent resides.

1–20

Pleadings

Proceedings must be begun within three years of termination of the engagement.

1–21

The application is made by originating summons in the High Court or originating application in the county court, with an affidavit in support. Where the application concerns the title to or possession of land, the originating summons or application must state whether the land is registered or not and, if so, the Land Registry Title number, and give details of any mortgage or other interest in the land. The affidavit must set out full details of the case.

The application and affidavit are served on the respondent with an acknowledgment of service. If contested, the respondent must file an affidavit in answer within 14 days of the time allowed for sending the acknowledgment of service.

Any mortgagee should be served and may apply to intervene.

Directions

If the respondent fails to respond within the time allowed, the applicant can seek a direction that the Respondent be debarred from defending the application unless an affidavit is filed within a specified time.

1–22

The court can order discovery or production of any documents, the filing of further affidavits, valuations, inquiries as to the whereabouts of money or property formerly in the possession or control of the respondent, the attendance of anyone and the taking of oral evidence.

A district judge can grant an injunction ancillary to or incidental to the relief sought. A district judge can refer an application or any question arising to a Judge.

Order

1–23 The court can make an order declaring or enforcing proprietory rights including orders for sale, return or restitution as thought fit. The court can order the payment of a lump sum equivalent to the value of an assessed interest.

The Precedents

C1. Originating Summons Under Section 17 of the Married Women's Property Act 1882

IN THE HIGH COURT OF JUSTICE   No.

    DIVISION

    DISTRICT REGISTRY

IN THE MATTER OF an application by   under s.17
Married Women's Property Act 1882

BETWEEN

                                                             Applicant

                        and

                                                          Respondent

LET   of

attend before *[Master/District Judge   in Chambers at the Principal Registry, Somerset House, Strand, London WC2R 1LP (or as the case may be)]*

on   day the   day of   19

at   o'clock in the   noon on the hearing of an application by the Applicant for an order in the following terms:-

1. That it should be declared that the property at *[address]* registered at H.M. Land Registry Title No. *[number]* and subject to a mortgage dated the *[date]* made between the Respondent of the one part and the *[name]* Building Society of the other part is owned by the Applicant absolutely or such order as to the ownership thereof as the court thinks fit

2. That the property be sold and the net proceeds of sale be divided equally between the Applicant and Respondent or otherwise as the court thinks fit

3. That it should be declared that the items numbered 1–10 inclusive in the Schedule attached hereto are the property of the Applicant

4. That it should be declared that the items numbered 11–20 inclusive in the Schedule are the joint property of the Applicant and the Respondent and should be divided between them as the court thinks fit

5. That the Respondent do deliver to the Applicant or his/her agent such items as are found to be the property of the Applicant within 7 days of the date of the order

6. That the Respondent should pay the costs of these proceedings

SCHEDULE

Dated the   day of

This summons was taken out by   of
Solicitors for the above named Applicant whose address is

To the Respondent:

TAKE NOTICE THAT:

1. A copy of the affidavit to be used in support of the application is delivered herewith

2. You must complete the accompanying Acknowledgment of Service and send it so as to reach the court within 8 days after you receive this summons

3. If you wish to dispute the claim made by the Applicant you must file an affidavit in answer within 14 days after the time allowed for sending the Acknowledgment of Service

4. If you intend to instruct a solicitor to act for you, you should at once give him all the documents served on you, so that he may take the necessary steps on your behalf

C2. Affidavit in Support of Section 17 of the MWPA Application

Applicant
[name]
1st
[date]

[*Heading as C1 above*]

I *[name]* of *[address and occupation or description]* the above named Applicant make oath and say as follows:

1. I met the Respondent in August *[year]* and on the 30th September *[year]* we became engaged to marry.

2. Soon after we became engaged we decided to purchase a property known as *[address]* which we intended should be our matrimonial home. I was completing a course of study in physiotherapy at the time and not earning an income. I therefore believed the Respondent when he told me that the Building Society insisted that the mortgage was in his sole name and the property was conveyed into his sole name. However he told me that he intended that I should have the house as my own property because he already owned another property in Florida of similar value and he wanted me to feel secure.

3. The purchase price was £225,000 of which £150,000 was provided by way of mortgage with the *[name]* Building Society, £25,000 was provided by me from an inheritance I had received in *[year]*, £25,000 was provided by my parents *[name]* and *[name]* of *[address]* and the balance was provided by the Respondent. I paid all the solicitors' costs and disbursements from my savings.

4. The conveyance was dated the 29th December *[year]* and we moved in on the 2nd January *[year]*. We lived there together until 9th May *[year]* when the Respondent left me and our engagement was terminated.

5. My physiotherapy course finished at the end of December *[year]* and I took up employment with the *[name]* Clinic with effect from the 9th January *[year]* earning £ *[number]* per month net rising to £ *[number]* per month net by January *[year]*. I contributed my earnings to the general housekeeping expenses and mortgage repayments even though the Respondent actually paid the mortgage payments to the Building Society. When we first moved in, the Respondent was working as an insurance salesman on a commission only basis and so his earnings varied greatly from month to

month. Some months he earned very little at all and other months he earned as much as £ *[number]*. If I had not been contributing to the general household expenses, I believe that the Respondent would not have been able to maintain the mortgage payments.

6. During *[year]* I suggested and the Respondent agreed that I should use the remaining £30,000 of my inheritance on having an outside swimming pool built. This was completed by June *[year]* and I believe that it has enhanced the value of the property.

7. The Respondent left me on the 9th May *[year]* and since then I have continued to live in the property and to make the mortgage payments myself. I therefore ask this Honourable Court to declare that the property is owned by me absolutely or to make such order relating thereto as the court thinks fit.

8. There is now produced and shown to me marked "*AB* 1" a Schedule and items 1–10 are presents given to me by my relatives and friends. I claim to be entitled to these absolutely.

9. Items 11–20 on the said Schedule were bought at various times during our relationship from our joint monies and I claim to be entitled to these items jointly with the Respondent.

SWORN at
in the County of
this   day of

BEFORE ME

C3. Affidavit in Answer to Section 17 of the MWPA Application

Respondent
[name]
1st
[date]

[Heading as C1 above]

I *[name]* of *[address and occupation or description]* the above named Respondent make oath and say as follows:-

1. I am the Respondent herein and I make this affidavit in response to the Applicant's claim under s.17 Married Women's Property Act 1882 and her affidavit sworn on the *[date]*

2. I refer to paragraphs 1 and 2 of the said affidavit and whilst it is true that from January *[year]* until May *[year]* we lived together in my house at *[address]*, I never agreed to marry the Applicant. Her parents did not approve of us living "in sin" as they put it and they exerted a great deal of pressure on us to marry. When we decided to live together they threw a party for us at which they indicated to their friends and relations that we were going to marry and the Applicant wore an engagement ring left to her by her grandmother.

Also it is not true to say that I told the Applicant that I intended her to have the house and it is not true to say that the mortgage was taken in my sole name at the insistence of the Building Society.

3. I refer to paragraph 3 of the said affidavit. The Applicant did provide £25,000 towards the purchase price but this was provided as a loan to me. I did offer to repay her in July *[year]* but she refused. The Applicant's parents did provide £25,000 but this was a gift. There was never any mention of them wanting it back until after I had left the Applicant and they wrote to me on the 13th June *[year]* claiming the payment had been a loan and demanding repayment. Whilst it is true to say that the Applicant paid the solicitors' charges I gave her the money for them.

4. I refer to paragraph 5 of the said affidavit. I do not know how much the Applicant was earning whilst we were living together. She always refused to tell me and kept her finances separate from mine. What I do know is that I paid every household bill during the time we were together and I made every mortgage payment. The Applicant did not contribute in any way at all other than to buy our

food. I believe that she spent the rest of her earnings on clothes and jewellery as she was always buying expensive new items. I was an insurance salesman at the time and I did struggle to make the payments occasionally but the Applicant never helped and I had to borrow from my parents.

5. I refer to paragraph 6 of the said affidavit. The Applicant did have a swimming pool built but this was strictly against my wishes. I do not swim. The Applicant liked to have her friends round for swimming parties. In view of the high costs of heating and cleaning the pool, I believe that it is a liability rather than an asset and has not enhanced the value of the house.

6. I refer to paragraph 7 of the said affidavit. I left the Applicant in May *[year]* because I was finding it increasingly difficult to manage the outgoings on the house and she would not discuss it with me or try to help. I thought that if I moved out she would realise how serious the problem was but she simply moved a new boyfriend in. I believe that this man, known to me as Sam, had moved in before the end of May and I believe that she must have been associating with him before I left. I was made redundant in July *[year]* and I have not been employed since.

7. I refer to paragraph 8 of the said affidavit. I accept that the items 1-10 in the Schedule exhibited to the said affidavit belong to the Applicant.

8. I refer to paragraph 9 of the said affidavit. I do not understand how the Applicant can say that items 11-20 in the Schedule were purchased from joint monies as we did not have any joint account. Items 11 and 12 and 16-20 were purchased by me and items 13 and 15 were given to me by my parents. I believe item 14 may have been purchased by the Applicant.

9. In all the circumstances I ask this Honourable Court to dismiss the Applicant's claim for the house or an interest in it and to dismiss her claim for items 11-13 and 15-20 or a share of them.

SWORN at
in the County of

this   day of

BEFORE ME

C4. Order under Section 17 of the MWPA 1882

[Heading as C1 above]

UPON THE APPLICATION of *[name]* and upon hearing Counsel for the Applicant and the Respondent and upon reading the Applicant's affidavit sworn the *[date]* and the Respondent's affidavit sworn the *[date]*

IT IS DECLARED that the freehold property at *[address]* is held by the Applicant and the Respondent upon trust to sell or retain the same and upon trust for themselves as tenants in common and that the beneficial interest of the Applicant in the property is 25 per cent and the beneficial interest of the Respondent is 75 per cent

AND IT IS ORDERED that the property be sold by private treaty at the best price reasonably obtainable and that after redemption of the mortgage in favour of the *[name]* Building Society and payment of the costs of sale the proceeds of sale be divided as to 25 per cent to the Applicant and as to 75 per cent to the Respondent

AND IT IS ORDERED that there be no order for costs save that the Respondent's costs be taxed on a legal aid basis

AND IT IS ORDERED that the parties be at liberty to apply

Dated the   day of

D. Application to Enforce Cohabitation Contracts or Separation Deeds

THE LAW

1–24 There is no statutory guidance on the enforceability of cohabitation agreements, but provided they are made at arm's length by parties of equal bargaining power in the full knowledge of all the relevant facts and with independent legal advice, they are likely to be upheld. They used to be considered void as contrary to public policy for sexual immorality but this is not now likely to be the case so long as the agreement is not simply for money in return for sex. There must clearly be an intention to create legal relations and so the agreement should use precise language to this effect. There must also be consideration for the agreement and this requirement is satisfied if the agreement is in the form of a deed. It is unlikely that the court would enforce matters of a personal nature, such as who is to do the washing or cleaning. However, matters of a financial nature can be enforced with an order for specific performance.

THE PROCEDURE

Court

1–25 An action may be commenced in the High Court—Chancery or Queen's Bench Division—or in the county court.

Pleadings

1–26 The statement of claim on a writ of summons in the High Court and the particulars of claim with a fixed date action in the county court should identify the agreement relied on, recite the covenants of which it is alleged the defendant is in breach, and give full details of how the defendant is in breach. It should also set out all forms of relief claimed as judgment can only be given for relief claimed.

Directions

1–27 The court may give directions for the filing of further pleadings if necessary, discovery and inspection, interrogatories, expert evidence and setting down.

Order

1–28 The order will start with a declaration as to the plaintiff's right to relief and that the agreement between the parties should be specifically performed. Consequential relief will depend on the nature of the contract. Damages may be awarded for breach of contract generally in lieu of specific performance or in addition to it. Damages will not be awarded in lieu if specific performance could not possibly have been ordered. An injunction can be granted as can rectification of the agreement or a declaration that the agreement has been repudiated. If the defendant fails to fulfil the terms of the judgment, the plaintiff can apply for an order that the order for specific performance be rescinded, the other party's repudiation accepted and damages awarded.

The Precedents

D1. Action to Enforce Covenants in a Cohabitation Contract

Endorsement on a Writ

The Plaintiff's claim is for:

(1) Specific performance of covenants contained in a (cohabitation contract) (separation deed) dated the *[date]* and made between the Plaintiff and the Defendant

(2) An injunction to restrain the Defendant, whether by himself or his servants or agents or otherwise, from *[give details of action(s) to be restrained]*

(3) Further or other relief

IN THE HIGH COURT OF JUSTICE   No.
    DIVISION
    DISTRICT REGISTRY

BETWEEN

Plaintiff

and

Defendant

STATEMENT OF CLAIM

1. The Plaintiff and Defendant lived together at *[address]* a property conveyed to them by a transfer dated the *[date]* as beneficial joint tenants in equal shares.

2. The parties entered into a cohabitation contract dated the *[date]*

3. By clause 9 the parties agreed to pay the common household expenditure equally

4. By clause 12 the parties agreed that items listed on the Schedule to the contract were considered to be owned by the Plaintiff

5. By clause 24(3) the parties agreed that if they both wished to remain in the property following the termination of the agreement then the first of them to provide evidence that a mortgage offer and/or cleared funds were available to that party should be able to purchase the other party's interest, such purchase to be completed

within one month thereafter. By clause 24(6) the parties agreed that if any party wishing to remain in the home is unable to complete the purchase within the specified period the home shall be sold.

6. From the *[date]* until the *[date]* of   when the Plaintiff vacated the property the Defendant ceased to pay one half of the common household expenditure in breach of the said clause 9 and instead made sporadic payments to the Plaintiff totalling £76.

7. On or about the *[date]* the Defendant removed the dining room table and chairs and the collection of Doulton figurines belonging to the Plaintiff from the property in breach of the said clause 12 and is believed to have disposed of the same for cash.

8. On the *[date]* the parties agreed to cease living together and the Defendant produced evidence that he had a mortgage offer to purchase the Plaintiff's interest in the home. The Defendant failed to complete the said purchase within one month or at all and refuses to sell the property in breach of clause 24(3) and (6)

AND the Plaintiff claims:

(1) Specific performance of the covenants contained in the cohabitation agreement

(2) An injunction to restrain the Defendant whether by himself or his servants or agents or otherwise from removing or disposing of any items listed in the Schedule to the agreement

(3) Further or other relief

Served this   day of
by

Solicitors for the Plaintiff

D2. Defence to Action to Enforce Covenants in a Cohabitation Contract

[*Heading as D1 above*]

DEFENCE

1. Paragraphs 1 to 5 of the Statement of Claim are admitted.

2. Save as is admitted below paragraph 6 of the Statement of Claim is denied.

The Defendant admits that he failed to pay one half of the household expenses as and when they fell due by virtue of his unemployment from the *[date]* to the *[date]*. He did pay £76 and when he gained employment he offered to reimburse the Plaintiff the balance of his share of the household expenses but this offer was refused. Clause 9 did not specify a time for payment and the Defendant denies that he is in breach of the said clause.

3. Paragraph 7 of the Statement of Claim is denied. The dining room table and chairs and collection of figurines were stolen from the property by persons unknown.

4. Save as is admitted below paragraph 8 of the Statement of Claim is denied.

The Defendant admits that he obtained a mortgage offer to purchase the Plaintiff's share in the property. The offer was subject to a satisfactory survey. The survey revealed substantial subsidence and the need for underpinning and other construction work to be carried out. The Defendant cannot afford to have the said work done and it is unlikely that the property would sell until it is done.

5. In the premises the Defendant denies that the Plaintiff is entitled to the relief claimed or any relief.

Served this   day of
by

Solicitors for the Defendant

D3. Action to Enforce Covenants in a Separation Deed

[Heading as D1 above]

STATEMENT OF CLAIM

1. The Plaintiff and the Defendant lived together from the *[date]* until the *[date]*.

2. By a deed dated the *[date]* and made between the Plaintiff and the Defendant the parties covenanted that they would live separate and apart from the date of the deed and that they would not molest or interfere with each other and that the Defendant will deliver up the items listed on the schedule to the deed.

3. Since that date the parties have lived separate and apart.

4. On several occasions the Defendant has committed acts in breach of the agreement and has indicated an intention to continue doing so.

5. On or about the *[date]* the Defendant harassed the Plaintiff by constantly telephoning him every few minutes from about 11 p.m. until about 2.30 a.m. the following day.

6. On or about the *[date]* the Defendant sent intimate personal photographs of the Plaintiff to his employer and to his family causing the Plaintiff considerable embarrassment and upset.

7. The Defendant has indicated that he intends to return to the Plaintiff's house against his wishes and the Plaintiff believes that he will do so and will continue to molest or otherwise interfere with the Plaintiff unless restrained from doing so.

8. The Defendant has failed to deliver up to the Plaintiff the items listed on the schedule to the deed despite numerous requests to do so.

AND the Plaintiff claims:

(1) Specific performance of the covenants contained in the separation deed

(2) An injunction to restrain the Defendant whether by himself or his servants or agents or otherwise from molesting or otherwise interfering with the Plaintiff

(3) Further or other relief

Served this   day of
by
Solicitors for the Plaintiff

D4. Defence to an Action to Enforce Covenants in a Separation Deed

[Heading as D1 above]

DEFENCE

1. Paragraphs 1 to 3 inclusive of the Statement of Claim are admitted.

2. Save that the Defendant admits that he telephoned the Plaintiff on about three occasions on the evening of the *[date]* paragraphs 4 to 7 are denied. The telephone calls were made and the items listed on the schedule to the deed were not delivered up as a result of breaches of the deed of separation by the Plaintiff as set out below and not in breach of the Defendant's covenants as alleged or at all.

3. It was a term of the agreement that the Plaintiff should during the joint lives of himself and the Defendant pay to the Defendant periodical payments of £ *[number]* per month. The Plaintiff has failed to maintain the said periodical payments in breach of the terms of the agreement. At the time the telephone calls were made the Plaintiff was three months in arrear.

4. In the premises the Defendant denies that the Plaintiff is entitled to the relief claimed or any relief.

Served this   day of
by

Solicitors for the Defendant

D5. Order For Specific Perfomance

[Heading as D1 above]

UPON HEARING Counsel for the Plaintiff and for the Defendant

AND UPON READING the documents recorded on the Court file as having been read

IT IS ORDERED that the covenants by the Defendant contained in the agreement dated the *[date]* in the Statement of Claim be specifically performed and carried into execution

AND IT IS FURTHER ORDERED that the Defendant do on or before *[   ]*

AND IT IS FURTHER ORDERED that the Defendant do pay to the Plaintiff the sum of £ *[number]* by way of damages together with the Plaintiff's costs of this action such costs to be taxed if not agreed

AND IT IS FURTHER ORDERED that the Defendant be charged with an occupation rent in respect of the said property calculated at the rate of £ *[number]* per week from the *[date]* to a date to be fixed by the Court

AND the parties are to be at liberty to apply

DATED this   day of

                                                               Judge

E. Actions Under Schedule 1 to the Children Act 1989

THE LAW

1–29 Paragraph 1 of Schedule 1 to the Children Act 1989 enables the court to make an order for a transfer of property from one parent to another for the benefit of a child "of the relationship" or to such a child or for a settlement of property for the benefit of such a child. It is not possible to apply for the benefit of a child of a previous relationship. It appears from the reported cases that an outright transfer from a sole legal owner to a non-owning partner is less likely than some sort of reverter to the owner when the children cease to be dependent. "Schedule 1 to the Children Act 1989 should be regarded as requiring the court to do no more than provide for the children as dependants.": *T v. S (Financial Provision for Children)*.[23]

THE PROCEDURE

Court

1–30 The High Court and county courts have equal jurisdiction. The magistrates' courts have no power to make orders for settlement or transfer of property.

Pleadings

1–31 The application is made on Forms C1 and C10 with a statement of means on Form C10A by a parent or guardian of the child or the holder of a residence order. The applicant must lodge sufficient copies for the court and each respondent who will be the other parent and any person believed to be interested in or affected by the proceedings. The court will provide Forms C6 (notice to parties) and C6A (notice to non-parties) where appropriate, endorsed with the date of the directions appointment, and Form C7 (acknowledgment) and the applicant must serve these on each respondent in accordance with FPR 1991, r. 4.8 at least 14 days prior to the hearing or directions appointment. At the first appointment, the applicant must file Form C9 (statement of service). The respondent must file Form C7 within 14 days of service.

---

[23] [1994] 2 F.L.R. 883.

Directions

The Court can arrange a timetable for the filing of statements **1–32**
including the filing of a statement of means on Form C10A by the
respondent, and give such other directions as it thinks fit.

Order

The Court can order the payment of a lump sum or the settlement **1–33**
or transfer of property.

The Precedents

Form C1	Appendix, p. 158.
Form C6	Appendix, p. 165.
Form C6A	Appendix, p. 167.
Form C7	Appendix, p. 169.
Form C9	Appendix, p. 171.
Form C10	Appendix, p. 172.
Form C10A	Appendix, p. 175.

PART II: ACTIONS BY A SURVIVOR WHEN ONE PARTNER DIES

A. Claims Under The Inheritance (Provision for Family and Dependants) Act 1975

THE LAW

2–01 A surviving cohabitant can claim against a deceased partner's estate under the 1975 Act on the grounds that the deceased's will or the intestacy rules do not make reasonable financial provision for the maintenance of the applicant. The deceased must have died domiciled in England or Wales, though the actual place of death is irrelevant.

The following persons may apply:

(1) If the deceased died on or after January 1, 1996, any person who for the whole of the period of two years ending immediately before the death of the deceased, was living in the same household as the deceased as the husband or wife of the deceased.[1] A surviving cohabitant of the same sex as the deceased or who lived intermittently with the deceased will not qualify.

(2) A surviving cohabitant if he or she was, immediately before the death of the deceased, wholly or partly maintained by the deceased. Deciding whether someone has been wholly or partly maintained is a balancing act, *i.e.* has the deceased made a substantial contribution towards the applicant's reasonable needs otherwise than for valuable consideration?[1a]

---

[1] Section 1A of the Act inserted by section 2 of the Law Reform (Succession) Act 1995.
[1a] *Bishop v. Plumley* [1991] 1 All E.R. 236.

(3) A child of the deceased (adult or minor, but the court is less likely to be sympathetic to an adult child with no disability).[2]
(4) A child of the survivor who was not also a child of the deceased if he or she was, immediately before the death of the deceased, wholly or partly maintained by the deceased.

2–02 The court must have regard to the following:

(a) for applications under (1) above:
  (i) the age of the applicant and how long he or she and the deceased had been living together as husband and wife;
  (ii) the contribution made by the applicant to the welfare of the family of the deceased including the contribution made by looking after the home or caring for the family;
(b) the resources and needs of the applicants and beneficiaries;
(c) the obligations and responsibilities of the deceased;
(d) the size and nature of the estate;
(e) any physical or mental disability of any applicant or beneficiary;
(f) the extent to which and the basis upon which the deceased assumed responsibility for the applicant and for how long; and
(g) any other matter including the conduct of the applicant or any other person which, in the circumstances of the case, the court considers relevant.

THE PROCEDURE

Court

2–03 Proceedings may be begun in the High Court—Chancery or Family Division—or the county court. An action which has a quantifiable value of less than £25,000 must be tried in the county court unless the county court decides, taking account of the criteria set out below, that it ought to transfer to the High Court or the action was started in the High Court and the High Court decides that it should stay. If the action has a quantifiable value of £25,000 or

---

[2] See Re *Coventry (dec'd)* [1980] Ch. 461.

more, then it must be tried in the High Court unless it was started in the county court and it is decided that it should stay or the High Court decides that it should transfer. The criteria are:

(i) the financial substance of the action including the value of any counterclaim;
(ii) whether the action is otherwise important and, in particular, whether it raises questions of importance to people who are not parties or is of general public interest;
(iii) the complexity of the facts, legal issues, remedies or procedures involved;
(iv) whether transfer is likely to result in a speedier trial.

Application for transfer can be made by summons with evidence. Unless they consent, the parties must be given the opportunity of being heard before a transfer is made.

Pleadings

The application is made by originating summons in the High Court or by originating application in the county court with an affidavit in support exhibiting an official copy of the grant of representation and of every testamentary document admitted to proof.

2–04

The application must be made within six months of the issue of the grant of representation. (The entry of a standing search at the Principal Probate Registry will ensure notification of the issue of any grant and this can be renewed at six-monthly intervals.) Otherwise leave of the court is required and reasons for the delay must be given in the affidavit in support. If there is no member of the deceased's family available or willing to take a Grant, the Official Solicitor may be willing to do so to enable a cohabitee to make a claim against the estate.

The affidavit should set out details of the length of the cohabitation giving starting and finishing dates, state whether the parties lived together as husband and wife and, where appropriate, show how the deceased wholly or partly maintained the applicant. It should also give as much information as possible about the matters the court has to consider under (a) to (g) at 2–02 above and state why, in the applicant's opinion, the deceased's will or the rules of intestacy do not make reasonable financial provision for him or her.

Copies of the summons or application and affidavit must be served on every personal representative, beneficiary and any other person affected by the claim or directed by the court to be added. The acknowledgment of service must be filed within 14 days of service and affidavits in answer within 21 days of service.

Directions

2–05 Upon issue, a pre-trial review date must be fixed. The court can give directions for the filing of (further) affidavits, discovery and inspection, valuations and setting down.

Order

2–06 An order giving leave to apply more than six months after the issue of the grant of representation will normally be granted where it is reasonably clear that it is required in the interests of justice. Personal representatives who distribute an estate after six months are not personally liable if there is no application pending at the time of distribution. Any property already distributed may be recovered from the beneficiaries if it is required for a dependant who is successful with a late application.

The court may award such financial provision as would be reasonable in all the circumstances of the case for the applicant to receive for his maintenance. The court has power to make orders for periodical payments, lump sums, property transfers, settlement and acquisition of property and variation of ante-nuptial or post-nuptial settlements. Provision is made out of the deceased's net estate. The court may order property comprised in transactions made by the deceased with the intention of defeating claims to be made available for the purpose of meeting such claims. Property held by the deceased as a beneficial joint tenant may be treated as part of the net estate provided the application was made within six months of the grant of representation.[3]

---

[3] Inheritance (Provision for Family and Dependants) Act 1975, s. 9: *Jessop v. Jessop* [1992] 1 F.L.R. 591.

The Precedents

A1. Originating Summons Under the Inheritance (Provision for Family and Dependants) Act 1975

IN THE HIGH COURT OF JUSTICE   No.
CHANCERY DIVISION
    DISTRICT REGISTRY
IN THE MATTER OF THE INHERITANCE (PROVISION FOR FAMILY AND DEPENDANTS) ACT 1975
AND IN THE ESTATE OF *[NAME]* DECEASED
BETWEEN

                                       Plaintiff

        and

                                       Defendant

LET ALL PARTIES concerned attend before *[Master   at Chancery Chambers Room No.   , Thomas More Building, Royal Courts of Justice, Strand, London WC2A 2LL* or *District Judge   at District Registry at   ]* on   day the   day of   at   o'clock in the   noon on the hearing of an application by the Plaintiff:-

(1) for an Order that he/she be granted leave to make an application under the Inheritance (Provision for Family and Dependants) Act 1975 notwithstanding that a period of six months has expired since the issue of a Grant of Representation in regard to the estate of the above mentioned *[name]*

(2) for an Order that such reasonable provision as this Honourable Court thinks fit be made for the Plaintiff out of the net estate of the above mentioned *[name]*

(3) for such further or other relief as shall be just

(4) for an order that the costs of this application be paid out of the said estate

This application is made under the Inheritance (Provision for Family and Dependants) Act 1975

AND let the Defendant within 14 days after service of this summons on him/her counting the day of service, return the accompanying Acknowledgment of Service to the appropriate court office

Dated the   day of

NOTE: This summons may not be served later than 4 (or if leave to effect service out of the jurisdiction is required, 6) calendar months beginning with the above date unless renewed by the Order of this Court

This summons was taken out by   of
(Agents for   of   )
Solicitors for the Plaintiff

To the Defendant and to   of
his/her solicitors

NOTE: If a Defendant does not attend personally or by his/her Counsel or solicitor at the time and place above mentioned such order will be made as the court may think just and expedient

A Defendant who is a Personal Representative must within 21 days after service of this summons on him/her, inclusive of the day of service, lodge with the court an affidavit in answer, stating the particulars required by Order 99 rule 5 of the Rules of the Supreme Court

IMPORTANT
Directions for the Acknowledgment of Service are given with the accompanying form

A2. Affidavit in Support of Inheritance Act Claim

Plaintiff
[name]
1st
[date]

[Heading as A1 above]

I, *[Name]* of *[address and occupation and description]* make oath and say as follows:-

1. I am the Plaintiff herein and I make this affidavit in support of my application under the Inheritance (Provision for Family and Dependants) Act 1975 for reasonable financial provision for me out of the estate of *[name]*

2. I lived with the said *[name]* as husband and wife for the whole of the period from the *[date]* until the date of his death on *[date]*.

3. *[Name]* had made a will leaving the bulk of his estate to me but this will has been declared invalid because it was not signed and witnessed properly. Under the rules of intestacy, the whole of his estate passes to his wife. To the best of my knowledge and belief, he had not seen or had any contact with his wife for ten years. He told me and I believed that she was an extremely wealthy woman, that she had resisted divorce in the early years of their separation and he had not bothered since.

4. When I met the deceased I was employed as features editor on a national women's magazine earning a very good salary. He asked me to go and live with him in his house at *[address]* and to give up my job so that I could devote my time to supporting him in his business, helping him to entertain clients and looking after the home. I agreed. From then on, he opened a joint account and I drew from this any money I needed for such things as housekeeping, entertaining, decorating or household furnishings, clothing, hairdressing, cosmetics and cleaning. He paid all the household bills. I did write the occasional feature for magazines on a freelance basis for which I received a modest fee but I was predominantly dependant on the deceased.

5. At the date of his death, he owned his house which I understand to be worth approximately £ *[number]*. He had a mortgage protection policy which has cleared the mortgage. He also owned the contents of the house which I understand to be worth approximately £ *[number]*.

In addition, I believe that he had the following assets:-
[number] shares in *[name]* worth approximately £ *[number]*
[number] shares in *[name]* worth approximately £ *[number]*
[number] shares in *[name]* worth approximately £ *[number]*
A 40ft yacht named *[name]* worth approximately £ *[number]*
A life insurance policy with *[name]* Assurance Company worth approximately £ *[number]*
A life insurance policy with *[name]* Assurance Company worth approximately £ *[number]*
A pension with *[name]* which paid out a lump sum on death in service and also widow's benefits but I have not been able to ascertain the details.
A bank account with *[name]* Bank holding approximately £ *[number]*
An account with the *[name]* Building Society holding approximately £ *[number]*

6. I was extremely shocked and upset by the sudden nature of the death of the deceased and I found it very difficult to come to terms with it. When I discovered that his will was invalid and that despite living as his wife for all those years I had no right to any part of his estate, I suffered a nervous breakdown. I went to live with my mother and I was not aware that the deceased's wife had taken out a Grant of Representation.

7. I am now recovering and two months ago I consulted solicitors who advised me to apply for legal aid to make this claim. They discovered that the Grant of Representation had been issued and there is now produced and shown to me marked "*AB*1" a true copy of the said Grant. I ask this court to give me permission to make this claim even though more than six months has expired. The delay was due to my illness.

8. I am now trying to find a way of earning a living but my recent attempts at writing have all been rejected. I may have to consider undertaking a training course. In the meantime I am claiming Income Support of £ *[number]* per week of which I give £ *[number]* to my mother for my keep. I have no savings, investments or assets whatsoever. The joint account I had with the deceased was frozen by the bank.

9. I therefore ask this Court to make reasonable financial provision for me out of the deceased's estate.

SWORN at
in the County of
this   day of

BEFORE ME

A3. Affidavit in Answer to Inheritance Act Claim

Defendant
[name]
1st
[date]

[Heading as A1 above]

I, *[name]* of *[address and occupation and description]* make oath and say as follows:-

1. I am the Defendant herein and I make this affidavit in answer to the Plaintiff's claim for reasonable financial provision from the deceased's net estate and her affidavit sworn on the *[date]*.

2. The deceased left me to live with the Plaintiff but he and I remained on very good terms until his death. I believe that he did not let the Plaintiff know he was in contact with me because she would have been angry and made a fuss. I met the Plaintiff once or twice in the early days and I formed the opinion that she was only interested in the deceased for his money. From those initial impressions and from various things the deceased told me over the years, I believe that she was very selfish and did not love him but he was besotted with her.

3. The deceased had told me that over the last two years before his death she had spent a decreasing amount of time with him. She had retained her association with her friends in the publishing world and had always stayed overnight in London at least once a week but during the last two years this had become more frequent. During the last six months I believe that there were weeks at a time when she did not return and she would just appear for parties to put on a show for him. On the last occasion she even brought a young man with her and spent the evening being very intimate with him in front of the deceased and his guests causing him much embarassment. The deceased was becoming more and more upset with the Plaintiff and I believe that it was the distress and depression caused by her behaviour that led to his untimely death.

4. The deceased was an intelligent man and would have ensured that any will was properly completed. If there was a will then I submit that either the Plaintiff wrote it or the deceased made it as a sham to keep the Plaintiff quiet without any intention of providing for her.

5. If the Plaintiff was dependant on the deceased during his lifetime then it was not out of necessity but out of choice. She had

a very succesful career as a features editor and she continued to work on a freelance basis throughout her time with the deceased. Articles regularly appeared under her name in various journals. I do not believe that the Plaintiff suffered a nervous breakdown and I put her to proof of this. If she is not working now then I believe that that is again a matter of choice.

6. My circumstances are that I own my home which is worth approximately £ *[number]* and is subject to a mortgage of £ *[number]* with the *[name]* Building Society. I work as a teacher earning £ *[number]* per annum. I have a car which is ten years old and is worth about £ *[number]* I have no other savings, investments or assets. The Plaintiff says that she believed I am a wealthy woman. My father is very wealthy and she might assume that one day I would inherit. However my mother died three years ago and my father has remarried. It is therefore likely that his new wife will inherit the bulk of his estate.

7. In all the circumstances I do not believe it would be right for the Plaintiff to be given any financial provision from the deceased's estate and I ask this court to dismiss her claim.

SWORN at
in the County of
this   day of

BEFORE ME

A4. Order Extending Time

[Heading as A1 above]

UPON THE APPLICATION of the Plaintiff by Originating Summons

AND UPON HEARING (Counsel or Solicitors) for the Plaintiff (and for the Defendant)

AND UPON READING the documents recorded in the Court file as having been read

IT IS ORDERED that the period of six months prescribed by the above mentioned Act be extended under the provisions of s.4 of the said Act until *[date]* being the date of the issue of the Originating Summons herein

AND IT IS FURTHER ORDERED that the rest of the said Originating Summons be adjourned with liberty to restore

A5. Interim Order

[Heading as A1 above]

UPON THE APPLICATION of the Plaintiff by Originating Summons

AND UPON HEARING (Counsel or Solicitors) for the Plaintiff (and for the Defendant)

AND UPON READING the documents recorded in the Court file as having been read

IT IS ORDERED that the Defendant as Personal Representative of the Deceased do pay to the Plaintiff by way of interim payments the sum of £ *[number]* per annum as from the *[date]* until further order the said sum to be paid by equal monthly instalments

AND (the Plaintiff and the Defendant by their Counsel undertaking to appear for cross examination on their respective affidavits) IT IS ORDERED that the said Originating Summons do stand adjourned to be heard in Court (with oral evidence) at   o'clock on   the   day of

AND the costs of this application are reserved.

A6. Order Under the Inheritance (Provision for Family and Dependants) Act

[Heading as A1 above]

UPON THE APPLICATION of the Plaintiff by Originating Summons

AND UPON HEARING (Counsel or Solicitors) for the Plaintiff (and for the Defendant)

AND UPON READING the documents recorded in the Court file as having been read

AND THE COURT being of the opinion that the disposition of the estate of the above named *[name]* effected by the Intestacy Rules is not such as to make reasonable provision for the maintenance of the Plaintiff

IT IS ORDERED that the Defendant as Personal Representative do pay to the Plaintiff on or before the *[date]* the sum of £ *[number]*

AND IT IS ORDERED that the costs of the Plaintiff and the Defendant be taxed on a standard basis and paid out of the estate of the above named

B. Actions to Resolve Disputed Succession to Private Tenancies

THE LAW

Housing Act 1988 assured tenancies

2–07   Where, immediately before a sole tenant's death, the tenant's spouse was occupying the property as his or her only or principal home and the tenant was not a successor, then the tenancy vests in the spouse and does not devolve under the tenant's will or intestacy. A person who was living with the tenant as his or her husband or wife shall be treated as the tenant's spouse and will succeed to the tenancy. There can be no succession if the deceased tenant was a successor and so where one of a married couple dies and the other succeeds to the tenancy, there can be no succession in favour of any new partner of the survivor. If more than one person qualifies as a "spouse", *e.g.* the tenant, his wife and the woman he lived with as husband and wife all shared the same home, then in default of agreement the court would decide.[4]

Rent Act 1977 tenancies

2–08   Where an original protected or stautory tenant dies after January 15, 1989 a spouse residing in the property immediately before the tenant's death becomes the stautory tenant so long as he or she continues to occupy it as his or her residence. A person who was living with the original tenant as his or her wife or husband shall be treated as the spouse of the original tenant. The cohabitation must have been settled, stable and permanent to qualify as living as husband and wife. If more than one partner qualifies and they cannot agree then the court decides.[5]

THE PROCEDURE

Court

2–09   Application is made to the county court for the district in which the respondent lives or carries on business or where the property is situated.

---

[4] s. 17(5) of the Housing Act 1988.
[5] Sched. 4, para. 2(3) of the Housing Act 1988, amending Sched. 1, para. 3 of the Rent Act 1977.

Pleadings

Proceedings are begun by originating application with affidavit in support setting out precise details of the living arrangements, with dates, of the applicant, the deceased tenant and the respondent, the personal circumstances of the applicant and any other relevant facts in support of the claim. **2–10**

Order

The court can make an order declaring who succeeds the tenancy under the relevant Act. **2–11**

The Precedents

B1. Originating Application to Ascertain Tenant on Death of Former Tenant

IN THE   COUNTY COURT   No.

(IN THE MATTER OF THE HOUSING ACT 1988)
(IN THE MATTER OF THE RENT ACT 1977)

BETWEEN:

Applicant

and

Respondent

[Name] of *[address and occupation]* applies to the Court for a Declaration relating to premises to which the said Act applies and situated at *[address]* of which *[name]* who died on the *[date]* day was tenant at the date of his death

The Applicant lived with the said *[name]* as his/her husband/wife and seeks an Order of the Court determining that he/she is the tenant of the said premises under the provisions of (section 17 Housing Act or section 2(1)(b) Rent Act)

AND for an Order providing for the costs of this application

The name and address of the person upon whom it is intended to serve this application are *[name and address]*

DATED this   day of

Solicitor for the Applicant

B2. Affidavit in Support of Application to Ascertain Tenant

Applicant
[name]
1st
[date]

[*Heading as B1 above*]

I *[name]* of *[address and occupation and description]* make oath and say as follows:-

1. I am the Applicant herein and I make this affidavit in support of my application for the court to determine whether I should succeed to the tenancy of the property known as *[address]*.

2. The tenant *[name]* was an (assured or protected/statutory tenant) of the said premises prior to his death on the *[date]* by virtue of an agreement made between him and *[name]* dated *[date]*.

3. The tenant was married to the Respondent and they lived in the said premises as their matrimonial home for two years before I met him. The marriage broke down and the tenant invited me to go and live with him. I met his wife and we got on really well together. She accepted that the marriage was over and bore me no ill will. She had nowhere else to go and so the tenant asked me if I minded if she stayed. I did not.

4. We all lived under the same roof for the next five years until the tenant's death. The tenant and I lived as husband and wife and on the *[date]* I gave birth to a daughter of whom the tenant was the father. The respondent and I shared the housework and the tenant paid all the bills.

5. I am unable to obtain paid employment until my daughter is of school age and so it would be difficult for me to find alternative rented accommodation. The council might be able to house me but I fear that the accommodation they would offer would not be suitable for me and my daughter. The respondent has already found employment and is free to take on another tenancy wherever

she likes. I therefore submit that I have a greater need to succeed to this tenancy.

SWORN at
in the County of
this   day of

BEFORE ME

B3. Order Determining Tenancy

[Heading as B1 above]

UPON HEARING the solicitors for the Applicant and for the Respondent

IT IS DETERMINED AND DECLARED pursuant to (section 17 Housing Act 1988 or section 2(1)(b) Rent Act 1977) that by reason of the death on the *[date]* of *[name]* who at the date of his death was the tenant of premises to which the Act applies known as *[address]* the said Applicant is the tenant of the said premises within the meaning of the said Act

DATED the   day of

C. Applications for a Beneficial Interest and/or Order for Sale

2–12 If a surviving cohabitant held a beneficial interest in a property with the deceased as tenant in common and refuses to sell (or the executors and trustees of the deceased's estate refuse to sell), then either side can make an application under section 14 of the Trusts of Land and Appointment of Trustees Act 1996 (TLATA) for an order for sale. An action may be brought for an order directing any act to be done in the administration of the estate or in the execution of a trust which the court could order if the estate or trust were being administered or executed under the direction of the court, *i.e.* the court can order a sale of property belonging to the estate or trust without ordering administration.

The same factors apply as in Part I, Section A and the applicant must be able to show that the purpose of the trust has come to an end. The precedents in Part I, Section A can be used making the executors and trustees of the deceased's will, or the personal representatives if there was no will, parties to the action.

If the beneficial ownership of joint owners is not clear, or if the size of the surviving cohabitant's share was not expressly declared in the title documents or, if the property was in the sole name of the deceased and the surviving cohabitant believes that he or she can establish entitlement to a beneficial interest on trust principles or proprietory estoppel, then he or she can apply to the court under section 14 of the TLATA to declare the extent of that interest.

The same factors apply as in Part I, Section A and the same precedents can be used making the personal representatives parties to the action.

D. Actions to Resolve Disputes About Guardianship

THE LAW

2–13 An unmarried father does not acquire parental responsibility on the mother's death unless she has appointed him to be the child's guardian. If he had already acquired parental responsibility during her lifetime then he will continue to exercise that responsibility to the exclusion of any guardian appointed by the mother. That guardian's appointment is postponed for so long as the father has parental responsibility. If, however, the mother had a residence order in her favour alone in force immediately before her death, her appointment of a guardian is effective immediately and parental responsibility is shared by the father and the guardian.[6]

If there is a disagreement about the exercise of parental responsibility, either the father or the guardian can apply for a relevant section 8 order (see Part III). If the disagreement is about the actual appointment as guardian, either can apply for the guardianship to be terminated.[7] The guardian can apply for an unmarried father's parental responsibility order or parental responsibility agreement to be terminated[8] or for a residence order to be discharged.[9] The usual welfare principles of the Children Act apply. An unmarried father can apply to the court to be appointed guardian as can anyone else.[10]

THE PROCEDURE

2–14 *For applications under section 8 of the Children Act 1989, see Part III.*

Court

2–15 Applications for the appointment or removal of a guardian can be made to any court and proceedings can be transferred sideways, upwards or downwards.

Pleadings

2–16 Application is made on Form C1. For an application for removal, there must be enough copies for each respondent and notice in Form C6 must be served on every person with parental responsibility, every person with parental responsibility before a care

---

[6] ss. 2(6), 5(6) of the Children Act 1989.
[7] s. 6(7).
[8] s. 4(3).
[9] ss. 8(2), 10(4)(a).
[10] s. 5(1)(a).

order and, on applications to discharge a court-appointed guardian, every party to the original proceedings. Notice in Form C6A must be served on the local authority if providing accommodation and any person caring for the child or providing refuge. If the application is for appointment, notice in Form C6A must be given to a father without parental responsibility. In the High Court or county court, a respondent may file a written answer.

Service

2–17 The applicant must serve a copy of the application and Form C6 endorsed with the date fixed for the hearing, or Form C6A endorsed with the date fixed for the hearing, on the relevant people described above, at least 14 days before the hearing. At or before the first directions appointment or hearing, the applicant must file a statement of service in Form C9. Any answer must be served not less than two days before the hearing.

Directions

2–18 Directions can be given for timetabling, submission of evidence, attendance and transfer.[11] A written request for directions must be made on Form C2.

Order

2–19 The appointment or removal of a guardian is made on Form C46. An appointment immediately vests the appointee with parental responsibility which continues unless and until terminated by the court. A removal immediately brings to an end the appointment of a guardian whether made by the court or not.

THE PRECEDENTS

Form C1	Appendix, p. 158.
Form C2	Appendix, p. 163.
Form C6	Appendix, p. 165.
Form C6A	Appendix, p. 167.
Form C9	Appendix, p. 171.
Form C46	Appendix, p. 187.

---

[11] See rr. 4.14(2), 4.15, 4.16 of the Family Proceedings Rules 1991 and r. 14(2), 15 and 16 of the Family Proceedings Courts (Children Act 1989) Rules 1991.

E. Fatal Accidents Act 1976 Applications

THE LAW

The deceased's dependants may bring an action against the person who, by any wrongful act, neglect or default is responsible for causing the death. Dependants include a person who lived with the deceased in the same household immediately before the date of death and had been living with the deceased as husband and wife in the same household for at least two years before the date of death[12] and any child of the deceased.[13] To bring an action, it must be shown first that if the deceased had not died, he or she would have been able to bring an action for damages. If there was contributory negligence on the part of the deceased, then the amount of damages recoverable will be reduced accordingly. **2-20**

The action is brought by the personal representatives but if there are no personal representatives or if no action is brought within six months of the date of death, the action may be brought by all or any of the dependants. It is only possible to bring one action and so all dependants should be included. It is normal for letters of administration to be taken out by the dependants for the purpose of bringing the action. The costs of securing the grant are usually allowed as part of the costs of the action.

THE PROCEDURE

Court

The action is begun in the Queen's Bench Division of the High Court or in the county court. The same criteria for transfer apply as for Inheritance Act claims under Section A above. **2-21**

Pleadings

The action is begun by writ of summons in the High Court. If the claim is extremely straightforward, the claim can be endorsed on the writ. Otherwise there should be a separate statement of claim. **2-22**

Directions

Directions can be given for further and better particulars of claim and defence, interrogatories, the exchange of witness statements if liability is in issue, exchange of medical reports on the dependant if **2-23**

---

[12] s. 1(3)(b).
[13] s. 1(3)(e).

relevant in assessing the multiplier, for filing of schedules of special damages, discovery and inspection and setting down.

Order

2–24 If damages are awarded, they are assessed in proportion to the dependant's injury resulting from the death. The court takes into account the fact that the cohabitant had no enforceable right to financial support. Reimbursement of funeral expenses can be ordered. After deducting costs not recovered from the defendant, damages are divided among the dependants in such shares as the court thinks fit.

If all the dependants are *sui juris*, the claim may be compromised or settled by simple agreement. If the dependant is under a disability, the compromise or settlement must be approved by the court.

THE PRECEDENTS

E1. Particulars of Claim

IN THE HIGH COURT OF JUSTICE   No.
QUEENS BENCH DIVISION
    DISTRICT REGISTRY

BETWEEN:

[Name] Personal Representative of *[Name]* deceased

Plaintiff

and

Defendant

STATEMENT OF CLAIM

1. The Plaintiff is *[describe relationship to deceased]* and brings this action under the Fatal Accidents Act 1976 for the benefit of the deceased's dependants. (Probate was granted by the *[name]* Probate Registry on the *[date]*.

2. At all material times the deceased was employed by the Defendants as *[job title]* at *[address]*

On the *[date]* *[describe accident]*. The deceased died from the injuries sustained in that accident on the *[date]*.

3. The deceased's death was caused by the negligence and or breach of statutory duty of the Defendants, their servants or agents.

PARTICULARS

[Give particulars of Defendants' negligence and/or breach of statutory duty]

4. By reason of the Defendants' said negligence and/or breach of statutory duty the deceased's dependants and estate have suffered loss and damage.

PARTICULARS PURSUANT TO STATUTE

(a) The persons for whose benefit this action is brought are:-

    (1) the Plaintiff, his cohabitant of *[number]* years now aged *[number]*

    (2) *[Name]* his child born on the *[date of birth]*

both of whom were dependant on the deceased at the time of his death.

(b) the nature of the claim is that the deceased who was aged *[number]* at the time of his death was a strong healthy man who had worked continuously for the defendants since *[date]*. His take home pay averaged around £ *[number]* a substantial part of which was spent for the benefit of the said dependants who all lived together in the same household and this would have continued had he remained alive. The deceased was the principal income producer for the family.

(c) the funeral expenses were £ *[number]*
[Add any special damages]

AND the Plaintiff claims

(1) damages under the Fatal Accidents Act 1976 for the benefit of the deceased's dependants
(2) damages under the Law Reform (Miscellaneous Provisions) Act 1934
(3) interest on such damages pursuant to section 35A Supreme Court Act

Served the   day of
by
Solicitors for the Plaintiff

PART III: ACTIONS RELATING TO CHILDREN

A. Actions to Resolve Disputes About Paternity

THE LAW

If there is any dispute about paternity of a child and the parties cannot agree to DNA profiling of blood samples, then the court has the power to direct DNA testing if paternity will have a bearing on some other issue, *i.e.* residence, contact or maintenance, and it is in the child's interest. The power is one of discretion and not compulsion and so anyone over 16 can refuse to be tested. A refusal entitles the court to draw adverse inferences (see *Re A (A Minor) (Paternity: Refusal of Blood Test*[1]*)*. **3–01**

Application is made to the court hearing the particular issue or the court makes the direction of its own motion. Blood tests are then carried out in accordance with the Blood Tests (Paternity) Regulations 1971, the Blood Tests (Evidence of Paternity) Regulations 1971 and the Magistrates Court (Blood Tests) Rules 1977.

Apart from this, section 22 of the Family Law Reform Act 1987 enables a child to apply to the court for a declaration that a man who is not married to the child's mother is or was the child's father. A man cannot seek a declaration that a child is his child because this is better resolved in the context of any issue over, for example, residence or maintenance. Under section 27 of the Child Support Act 1991 the Secretary of State for Social Services or the parent with care of the child can apply to the court for a declaration as to whether or not the alleged parent is the parent.

---

[1] [1994] 2 F.L.R. 463.

The Procedure

Court

3–02 Application under the Family Law Reform Act is made to the High Court Family Division or to a county court where the applicant is domiciled in England and Wales on the date of application or has been habitually resident in England and Wales for a period of one year ending with that date.

Application under the Child Support Act is made to the magistrates court, though it can be transferred upwards.

Pleadings

3–03 Application under the Family Law Reform Act is made by petition with an affidavit by the petitioner or, if under 18, by a next friend, verifying the facts in the petition and giving details of anyone whose interest may be affected by the proceedings and that person's relationship to the petitioner. A copy of the petitioner's birth certificate must be exhibited to the affidavit. The procedure is governed by rules 3.13 and 3.16 of the Family Proceedings Rules 1991. The petition must state:

- the petitioner's name and, if he or she is known by a name different from that shown on the birth certificate, that name, sex, date and place of birth;
- the full name of the father and his date and place of birth, his residence and occupation if known;
- the full name of the mother at her date of birth, at the date of her first marriage, at the date of birth of the petitioner, at the date of her most recent marriage and at the date of the presentation of the petition, the mother's date and place of birth and her residence and occupation;
- the grounds on which the petitioner relies and all other relevant facts to help justify the application;
- whether there have been any other proceedings in any court in England and Wales or anywhere relating to the parentage of the petitioner and, if so, the date begun, the names of the parties, the date or expected date of trial, the court, the nature, outcome or present state of the proceedings;
- that the petitioner is domiciled in England and Wales on the date of presentation or has been habitually resident for one year;
- his or her nationality, citizenship or immigration status and the effect that granting the declaration would have on that status.

Both parents are respondents to the petition.

Application under the Child Support Act is simply made in writing giving the details—there is no prescribed form.

Service

A Family Law Reform Act application must be served in accordance with rule 2.9 of the FPR. 3–04

For Child Support Act applications, no time for service is prescribed but it is reasonable to assume that 21 days' notice should be given. A written answer must be filed, indicating whether or not it is intended to defend, within 14 days of service.

Directions

With Family Law Reform Act applications, further respondents may be added by direction of the court after answers have been filed. The court can direct that all necessary papers be sent to the Attorney-General and the Attorney-General may intervene anyway. One month prior to the filing of the petition a copy of the petition and every accompanying document must be sent to the Attorney-General, and if he wishes to intervene he will notify the court. When all the answers have been filed, the petitioner must issue and serve on all the respondents a request for directions as to whether any other person should be made a respondent or given notice of the proceedings. The Attorney-General need not file an answer but must be directed to serve on all parties a summary of his argument. 3–05

If directions have been given that notice of proceedings be sent to anyone other than the respondents, such people can apply within 21 days of service to be joined as parties. Directions for trial will not be given until the time for filing an answer by the Attorney-General and for applying to be joined has expired.

The court can direct that the whole or part of the proceedings be held *in camera* and can direct blood tests.

For Child Support Act applications, the court may direct that the matter proceed as if it had started as an originating summons or application. Any document served or other thing done while the proceedings were pending in another court shall be treated as applicable to the court to which the matter has been transferred. A pre-trial hearing can be held to decide what directions, if any, should be given and these might include directions for blood tests. The application may be heard and determined by a district judge.

Order

With Family Law Reform Act applications, if satisfied that the alleged parent is the father then the court must issue a declaration unless to do so would be manifestly contrary to public policy. The 3–06 declaration binds everyone and the court notifies the Registrar General who can authorise the re-registration of birth of the child where appropriate.

An order made under the Child Support Act will clearly define liability for child support and the Agency will be able to proceed with assessments and enforcement under the provisions of the Act.

The Precedents

A1. Petition for Declaration as to Parentage

IN THE HIGH COURT OF JUSTICE   No.
FAMILY DIVISION
    DISTRICT REGISTRY

IN THE MATTER OF *[Petitioner's name]*
AND IN THE MATTER OF S.22 FAMILY LAW REFORM ACT 1987

The   day of

THE PETITION of *[name]* shows that:-

1. The Petitioner's full name is *[full name]*

2. The Petitioner is a male/female and was born on the *[date of birth]* at *[address]*

in the County of *[county]*

3. The Petitioner's father is/was *[full names]* who was born at *[address]* on the *[date]* and who resides/resided at *[address]* and whose occupation is/was *[occupation]*

4. The Petitioner's mother is/was *[full names]* who was born at *[address]* on the *[date]* and who resides/resided at *[address]* and whose occupation is/was *[occupation]*. The mother was known by the following names at the following times *(e.g. at birth, at first marriage, at birth of Petitioner, at second marriage, at date of petition)*

5. [The Petitioner is domiciled in England and Wales or has been habitually resident in England and Wales throughout the period of one year ending with the date of presentation of this petition]

6. That *[father's name]* and *[mother's name]* were living together at the date of the Petitioner's birth on the *[date]* and that *[father's name]* and *[mother's name]* were entered as the Petitioner's parents in an entry made on the *[date]* in the Register of Births for the Registration District of *[name]* wherein the Petitioner is called *[petitioner's name]* a copy of which is disclosed

7. There have been no previous proceedings in any court with reference to the parentage of the Petitioner by or on behalf of the Petitioner

THE PETITIONER THEREFORE PRAYS that the Court will declare that the said *[father's name]* and the said *[mother's name]* are/were the parents of the said Petitioner.

A2. Affidavit Verifying Facts in Petition

                                                              Petitioner

                                                               [name]

                                                                     1st

                                                               [date]

[*Same heading as A1 above*]

I *[Petitioner's name]* of *[address]* the above named Petitioner *[(name address and occupation) next friend of   ]* make oath and say as follows:-

1. The statements contained in paragraphs *[numbers]* of (the/my) petition herein are true

2. The statements contained in paragraphs *[numbers]* of (the/my) petition are true to the best of my information and belief *(state sources and grounds of information and belief)*

3. The following are the persons whose interests may be affected by these proceedings with their relationship to (the Petitioner/me): *List names, addresses, occupations and relationships*

4. There is now produced and shown to me marked "A" a true copy of my *(the)* birth certificate *(of the Petitioner)*

Sworn at
in the County of
this   day of

Before me

A3. Declaration of Parentage

[Same heading as A1 above]

UPON THE PETITION of *[name]* and upon hearing and upon reading

IT IS DECLARED that *[name]* is/was the parent of the said Petitioner

DATED the   day of

B. Applications for Parental Responsibility Orders

THE LAW

A child's mother has parental responsibility for the child. A child's unmarried father does not. He will only acquire parental responsibility by: **3–07**

(a) marrying the child's mother;
(b) entering into a parental responsibility agreement with the child's mother[2];
(c) obtaining a parental responsibility order under section 4 of the Children Act 1989[3];
(d) obtaining a residence order under section 8 of the Children Act 1989—when the court must make a parental responsibility order[4];
(e) being appointed guardian, in which case parental responsibility would become vested in him upon the mother's death[5];
(f) adopting the child.

On an application for a parental responsibility order under section 4, the general principles of the Act apply, *i.e.*:

(a) the welfare of the child is the paramount consideration;
(b) the making of an order must be better for the child than making no order at all.

The court will take into account the degree of commitment which the applicant had shown towards the child, the degree of attachment which existed between them and his reasons for applying for the order: Re H *(Illegitimate Children; Father; Parental Rights (2)*[6]*)*.

"Where you have a concerned though absent father who fulfils the test in *Re H* then prima facie it would be for the welfare of the child that a parental responsibility order be made": Balcombe L.J., *Re G (A Minor) (Parental Responsibility Order).*[7]

An order can be made in respect of any child under the age of 18.

---

[2] See Appendix 1, below.
[3] See below.
[4] s. 12(1)—see Section D, below.
[5] See Part V, Section E, below.
[6] [1991] 1 F.L.R. 214.
[7] [1994] 1 F.L.R. 504.

The Procedure

Court

3-08 Any court can make an order and proceedings can be transferred sideways, upwards or downwards.

Pleadings

3-09 Where paternity is in issue, that must be determined before the putative father can apply. The application is made on Form C1 giving all the information required by that form including the reasons for the application. The respondent to an application in the High Court or a county court, but not a family proceedings court, may file a written answer.

Service

3-10 The applicant must serve a copy of the application together with Form C6 for each respondent, *i.e.* every person the applicant believes to have parental responsibility and every person the applicant believes had parental responsibility prior to a care order being made, endorsed with the date fixed for the hearing, at least 14 days before the hearing.

The applicant must serve notice of the proceedings endorsed with the date fixed for hearing in Form C6A, but not the application, on any local authority providing accommodation for the child or any person with whom the child is living at the time the proceedings commenced or any person providing refuge where the child is alleged to be staying in a refuge, at least 14 days before the hearing. At or before the first directions appointment or hearing, the applicant must file a statement proving service in Form C9.

Directions

3-11 Directions can be given for the timetabling of the proceedings, the attendance of the child, the submission of evidence, preparation of a welfare report, transfer of proceedings, appointment of guardian *ad litem* or solicitor for the child. A written request for directions must be made on Form C2.

Order

3-12 The order, in Form C45 (Appendix, p. 186), confers parental responsibility on the father, *i.e.* he shares all the rights, duties, powers, responsibilities and authority which a parent has in relation to a child and his property with the mother. The order ends automatically when the child is 18 or when the child is adopted or the parents marry, unless previously discharged by the court.

The Precedents

> Form C1 .... Appendix, p. 158.
> Form C2 .... Appendix, p. 163.
> Form C6 .... Appendix, p. 165.
> Form C6A .... Appendix, p. 167.
> Form C9 .... Appendix, p. 171.
> Form C45 .... Appendix, p. 186.

C. Application for Discharge of a Parental Responsibility Order or Parental Responsibility Agreement

THE LAW

3–13 Anyone with parental responsibility can apply for an order or agreement to be set aside. The child can apply having first obtained the leave of the court. Leave will only be granted if the court is satisfied that the child has sufficient understanding to make the application. The general principle that the welfare of the child is paramount applies. The court must be satisfied that discharging the order or agreement is better for the child than not. The court cannot end a parental responsibility order while a residence order in favour of the father is still in force.

THE PROCEDURE

Court

3–14 Application can be made to any court

Pleadings, service, directions

3–15

All as Section B, above.

The order, in Form C45 (Appendix, p. 186), terminates the parental responsibility agreement or parental responsibility order.

D. Application for an Order Under Section 8 of the Children Act 1989

THE LAW

Residence orders

If both parents have parental responsibility and cannot agree where and with whom the child is to live, or if an unmarried father without parental responsibility wants the child to live with him against the mother's wishes, then application can be made for a residence order which settles who the child is to live with. If such an order is made, then the person in whose favour it is made will also be granted a parental responsibility order, which cannot be terminated while the residence order remains in force, and will continue even after a residence order is discharged until it is separately terminated. The order ceases to have effect if the parents live together for more than six months.[8] The court should not make a residence order once a child has reached 16 unless there are exceptional circumstances.[9] If the making of a residence order is opposed, the court must have regard to[10]: **3–16**

(a) the ascertainable wishes and feelings of the child concerned (in the light of his or her age and understanding);
(b) his or her physical, emotional and educational needs;
(c) the likely effect on the child of any change in circumstances;
(d) the child's age, sex, background and any characteristics which the court considers relevant;
(e) any harm the child has suffered or is at risk of suffering;
(f) how capable is each parent, and any other person the court considers relevant, of meeting the child's needs;
(g) the range of powers available under the Children Act.

Contact orders

If there is a dispute between parents about contact between parent and child, an application can be made for a contact order which requires the person with whom a child lives to allow the child to visit or stay with the person named in the order or for that person and the child otherwise to have contact with each other. Contact **3–17**

---

[8] s. 11(5).
[9] s. 9(7).
[10] s. 1(3).

orders can therefore deal with contact by letters, telephone calls, cards and presents as well as no contact. Contact orders do not confer parental responsibility. Again, orders cannot be made in respect of a child who has reached the age of 16 and any order will cease to have effect if the parents live together for more than six months.

Specific issue orders

3–18 Application can be made for a specific issue order which is an order giving directions for the purpose of determining a specific question which has arisen, or which may arise, in connection with any aspect of parental responsibility for a child. It is not intended as a substitute for a residence or contact order. It can deal with such matters as schooling or medical treatment.

Prohibited steps orders

3–19 Application can be made for a prohibited steps order which is an order specifying that no step which could be taken by a parent in meeting his or her parental responsibility for a child, and which is of a kind specified in the order, can be taken by any person without the consent of the court, *e.g.* an order that a parent should not remove a child from the United Kingdom where there is no residence order in force.

The general principles of the Act apply to all applications under section 8, *i.e.* the welfare of the child is paramount and the making of an order must be better for the child than not making an order.

THE PROCEDURE

Court

3–20 Application can be made to any court and proceedings can be transferred sideways, upwards or downwards. A district judge of the principal registry can hear any application for a section 8 order. A district judge in a county court can hear interlocutory matters, unopposed trials and some opposed trials in limited circumstances. A contact order cannot be made in respect of a child in care.

Applications to vary or discharge orders are made in the same way.

Pleadings

3–21 The action can be started as a free-standing application or application can be made in any family proceedings. The application is made on Form C1 giving all the information required by that

Application for an Order Under Children Act

form including the reasons for the application. The respondent to an application in the High Court or a county court, but not a family proceedings court, may file a written answer.

Service

The applicant must serve a copy of the application together with Form C6 endorsed with the date fixed for hearing, on every person with parental responsibility and every person with parental responsibility prior to a care order, at least 14 days before the hearing. Notice of the proceedings in Form C6A endorsed with the date fixed for hearing must be served on the local authority if providing accommodation for the child, any person caring for the child or providing refuge, any party to the pending proceedings and any person with whom the child has lived for three years.

At or before the first directions appointment or hearing, the applicant must file a statement of service in Form C9.

The court has power to abridge time.

The respondent must file an acknowledgement of the application in Form C7 and serve it on the parties within 14 days of service. A respondent filing a written answer must serve it on the other parties not less than two days before the hearing.

3–22

Directions

The court can give directions as to timetabling, submission of evidence, attendance at hearings and transfer of proceedings. A written request for directions must be made on Form C2.

3–23

Order

The order is made on Form C43 (Appendix, p. 184). It may contain directions and conditions and a penal notice may be attached on application in the High Court or county court. An order for no contact falls within the definition of a contact order.

3–24

The Precedents

```
Form C1   ......... Appendix, p. 158.
Form C2   ......... Appendix, p. 163.
Form C6   ......... Appendix, p. 165.
Form C6A  ........ Appendix, p. 167.
Form C7   ......... Appendix, p. 169.
Form C9   ......... Appendix, p. 171.
Form C43  ........ Appendix, p. 184.
```

E. Application to Change Child's Name or Remove from the United Kingdom

THE LAW

3–25 If a residence order is in force, no one can change the child's surname or remove him or her from the United Kingdom for more than a month without the written consent of every person with parental responsibility or the leave of the court. In the absence of a residence order, if a dispute arises, application would have to be made for a specific issue order or prohibited steps order depending on the circumstances.

THE PROCEDURE

3–26 The procedure is as for any application under the Children Act with the application being made on Form C1 and any order being made on Form C44 (Appendix, p. 185).

F. Application for an Adoption Order

THE LAW

An adoption order extinguishes the parental responsibility any person had for the child immediately before the making of the order and gives parental responsibility for a child to the adopters. Joint applications can only be made by married parents. Therefore unmarried parents can only make individual applications. An unmarried father could apply for an adoption order as a means of removing parental responsibility from the mother but the court would need to be convinced that this would be for the benefit of the child. More likely is the situation where the mother marries a man who is not the father of the child and she and the new husband jointly apply for an adoption order so as to give the new husband parental responsibility and to extinguish any parental responsibility the father had.

3–27

The father could seek to frustrate an adoption application by applying for a parental responsibility agreement order or a residence order. His application would then have to be heard with the adoption application and decided on the welfare principles of the Children Act. If he has a parental responsibility or order or has been appointed guardian by the mother or by the court, then his agreement to the making of an adoption order is necessary unless the court dispenses with it. If there are strong ties between unmarried father and child, the court is more likely to take account of his wishes than in the past when the advantage of removing the stigma of illegitimacy outweighed the disadvantage of severing links with the father.

Joint applications can only be made by married couples and so unmarried couples and same sex couples cannot jointly apply. Sole applicants must be over 21, unmarried (or married but the spouse cannot be found, cannot make an adoption application because of physical or mental ill health or they are living apart and the separation is likely to be permanent) and domiciled in the United Kingdom, the Channel Islands or the Isle of Man. The child must be at least 19 weeks old and under 18 and must have lived with the applicants for the preceding 13 weeks in the case of a parent, stepparent, relative or adoption agency or for 12 months in all other cases.

If the identity of an unmarried father without parental responsibility is known to an adoption agency involved in a case, then it must find out whether he intends to apply for parental responsibility or a residence order. Where an application is made to free a child for adoption, the reporting officer must interview anyone claiming to be the father.

If a father without parental responsibility is liable to maintain a child under an order or agreement, he must be made a respondent to the application.

THE PROCEDURE

Court

3–28 Application can be made to the Family Division of the High Court, divorce county court within the jurisdiction of which the child resides at the date of the application or the family proceedings court. Proceedings can be transferred sideways, upwards or downwards.

Pleadings

3–29 Application is made by originating summons or originating application in Form 6. The identity of the applicant can be kept confidential by use of a serial number. The applicant has to file three copies of the application, the birth certificate of the child or certificate of previous adoption, any document evidencing parental consent or, if application is being made to dispense with consent, three copies of a statement of facts, a copy of any freeing order, the marriage certificate of married applicants, a medical report on each applicant and the child and the relevant adoption agency must file a Schedule 2 report.

Service

2–30 The application must be served on each parent or guardian of the child, unless the child is free for adoption, any adoption agency with parental responsibility under a freeing order, any adoption agency involved in the adoption arrangements, any local authority to whom notice has been given, any local authority or voluntary organisation with parental responsibility or caring for the child, any person liable to maintain the child and the spouse of a married sole applicant. In the High Court, the child is also made respondent.

Directions

3–31 If the parent appears willing to consent to the adoption, a reporting officer is appointed. If not, a guardian *ad litem* is appointed. At least four weeks before the hearing, the court must consider all the documents and give directions.

Order

An adoption order gives parental responsibility to the adopters and **3–32**
extinguishes any previous parental responsibility and any earlier
court orders. The child is treated as if born to the adopters. The
order may contain such terms and conditions as the court thinks fit
and may postpone determination of the application and make an
interim parental responsibility order for a maximum of two years
on such terms as it thinks fit. An order can only be made if the
child is in attendance unless there are special circumstances. The
order must contain a direction to the registrar general to make an
entry in the Adopted Children's Register.

The Precedents

F1. Originating Summons or Originating Application for Adoption Order

IN THE HIGH COURT OF JUSTICE   No.
FAMILY DIVISION
       DISTRICT REGISTRY

OR IN THE   COUNTY COURT [1]

IN THE MATTER OF

BETWEEN

                                     Plaintiff/Applicant

and

                                   Defendant/Respondent

I/We, the undersigned *[name of applicant(s)]* wishing to adopt *[name]* [2], a child, hereby give the following particulars in support of my/our application.

PART 1
Particulars of the applicant(s)

1. Name and address etc.

Name of (first) applicant in full ....
Address [3] ....
Occupation ....
Date of birth ....
Relationship (if any) to the child ....
Name of the (second) applicant in full ....
Address ....
Occupation ....
Date of birth ....
Relationship (if any) to the child ....

2. Domicile [4]

I am/We are/One of us (namely   ) is domiciled in [England and Wales *or* Scotland *or* Northern Ireland *or* the Channel Islands *or* the Isle of Man].

3. Status [5]

[We are married to each other and our [marriage certificate *or* other evidence of marriage] is attached *or* I am [unmarried *or* a

widow *or* a widower *or* a divorcee] *or* I am applying alone as a married person and can satisfy the court that ....
....
....]

[4. I am applying alone for an adoption order in respect of my own child and can satisfy the court that the other natural parent ....
....
...............................](6)

[5. **Health** (7)

A report on my/our health, made by a registered medical practitioner on the .... day of ....
.... 19 ...., is attached.]

Part 2
Particulars of the child (8)

6. Identity etc.

The child is of the male/female sex and is not and has not been married. He/she [was born on the ....
day .... of .... 19 .... and is the person to whom the attached birth/adoption certificate relates] *or* [was born on or about the ..... day of ....
19 .... in ....]

He/She is a .... national

[7. **Health** (9)

A report on the health of the child, made by a registered medical practitioner on the .... day of
.... 19 .... is attached]

[8. The child is free for adoption pursuant to section 18 of the Adoption Act 1976, and I/We attach hereto the order of the .....
.... Court dated ...., to that effect. Parental responsibility was thereby vested in .... [and was transferred to .... by order of the .... court under section 21 of the Adoption Act 1976 on the .... day of ....].] (10)

[9. **Parentage etc.** (11)

The child is the child of ....
[whose last known address was ....
or deceased]
[and ....

whose last known address was ....
or deceased].]

[10. The guardian(s) of the child (other than the mother or the father of the child)
is/are ....
of ....
[and ....
of ....].] (12)

[11. **Parental Agreement** (13)

I/We understand that ....
[and ....
is/are willing to agree to the making of an adoption order in pursuance of my/our application].]

[12. I/We request the judge to dispense with the agreement of .....
.... [and ....]
on the grounds that ....
....
....
and there are attached hereto three copies of a statement of facts upon which I/We intend to rely.]

[13. **Care etc.**

The child is being looked after by ....
[who has/have parental responsibility for the child].] (14)

[14. **Maintenance** (15)

....
of ....
is liable [by virtue of an order made by the ....
court at .... on the .... day of ....,
or by an agreement dated the .... day of ....]
to contribute to the maintenance of the child.]

15. **Proposed Names**

If the adoption order is made in pursuance of this application, the child is to be known by the following names:
Surname ....
Other names ....

PART 3
General

16. The child has lived with me/us continuously since the ....
day of .... [and has accordingly had his/her home with me/us for the five years preceding the date of this application.] (16)

Application for an Adoption Order

17. The child was [placed with me/us for adoption on the .... day of .... by .... an adoption agency, *or* received into my/our home in the following circumstances ....].(16)

[18. I/We notified the .... Council on the .... day of .... of my/our intention to apply for an adoption order in respect of the child.](17)

19. No proceedings relating in whole or in part to the child have been completed or commenced in any court in England and Wales or elsewhere [except ....].(18)

20. I/We have not received or given any payment or reward for, or in consideration of the adoption of the child, for any agreement to the making of an adoption order, the transfer of the home of the child with a view to adoption or the making of any arrangements for adoption [except as follows:
....
....]

21. As far as I/we know, the only person(s) or body(ies) who have taken part in the arrangements for the child's adoption are(19) :
....
....

[22. For the purposes of this application reference may be made to .... of ....](20)

[23. I/We desire that my/our identity should be kept confidential, and the serial number of this application is ....](21)

[24. I/We intend to adopt the child under the law of or within ... . which is the country of my/our domicile, and evidence as to the adoption in that country is filed with this process.]

[25. I/We desire to remove the child from the British Isles for the purpose of adoption.]

I/We accordingly apply for [an adoption order *or* an order authorising a proposed foreign adoption] in respect of the child.
Dated this .... day of ....
Signature(s) ....
            ....

NOTES

(1) If the application is made to the county court, it may be made to any county court which has been designated as a divorce county court under section 33 of the Matrimonial and Family Proceedings Act 1984.

(2) (Heading) Enter the first name(s) and surname of the child as shown in any certificate referred to in paragraph 6 below; otherwise enter the first name(s) and surname by which the child was known before being placed for adoption.

(3) (Paragraph 1) Insert the address where the applicant has his or her home and the place (if different) where documents may be served upon him.

(4) (Paragraph 2) May be deleted if the application is for an order authorising a proposed foreign adoption.

(5) (Paragraph 3) Documentary evidence of marital status should be supplied. A married applicant can only apply alone if he or she can satisfy the court that his or her spouse cannot be found, or that they have separated and are living apart and that the separation is likely to be permanent, or that by reason of physical or mental ill health the spouse is incapable of making an application for an adoption order. Any documentary evidence on which the applicant proposes to rely should be attached to the application. The name and address (if known) of the spouse should be supplied, and the marriage certificate (or other evidence of marriage) should be attached.

(6) (Paragraph 4) State the reason to be relied upon, e.g. that the other natural parent is dead or cannot be found, or that there is some other reason, which should be specified, justifying his or her exclusion. Documentary evidence, e.g. a death certificate, should be supplied where appropriate.

(7) (Paragraph 5) A separate health report is required in respect of each applicant and the report must have been made before the date of the application. No report is required, however, if the child was placed for adoption with the applicant by an adoption agency, or if he or she is the child of the applicant or either of them.

(8) (Paragraph 6) If the child has previously been adopted a certified copy of the entry in the Adopted Children Register should be attached and not a certified copy of the original entry in the Register of Births. Where a certificate is not attached enter the place (including the country) of birth if known.

(9) (Paragraph 7) The report must have been made during the period of three months before the date of the application. No report is required, however, if the child was placed for adoption with the applicant by an adoption agency, or if he or she is the child of the applicant or either of them.

(10) (Paragraph 8) The order made by the court freeing the child for adoption and any order made under section 21 of the Adoption Act 1976 should be attached.

(11) (Paragraph 9) This paragraph and paragraphs 10–14 only apply if the child is not free for adoption. If the child has previously been adopted, give the names of his adoptive parents and not those of his natural parents. If the parents of the child were not married to each other at the time of his birth and the father has parental responsibility for the child, give details under paragraph 19 of the court order or the agreement which provides for parental responsibility.

(12) (Paragraph 10) Enter particulars of any person appointed by deed or will in accordance with the provisions of the Guardianship of Infants Acts 1886 and 1925, or the Guardianship of Minors Act 1971 and the Children Act 1989 or by a court of competent jurisdiction or under section 5 of the Children Act 1989 to be a guardian. Do not include any person who has the custody of the child only. Delete this paragraph if the child has no guardian.

(13) (Paragraphs 11 and 12) Enter either in paragraph 11 or 12 the names of the persons mentioned in paragraphs 9 and 10, except that in the case of a child whose parents were not married to each other at the time of his birth the father of the child should be entered only if he has parental responsibility of the child by virtue of a court order or by agreement or he has a residence order in respect of the child. Where it is sought to dispense with parental agreement enter in paragraph 12 one or more grounds set out in section 16(2) of the Adoption Act 1976.

(14) (Paragraph 13) This paragraph should be completed where the child is being looked after by a local authority or a voluntary organisation.

(15) (Paragraph 14) This paragraph should be completed where some person or body is liable to contribute to the maintenance of the child under a court order or agreement

(16) (Paragraphs 16 and 17) Under section 13 of the 1976 Act, an adoption order cannot be made unless the child has had his or her home with the applicants or one of them:

    (a)   for at least 13 weeks if the applicant or one of them is a parent, step-parent or relative of the child or if the child was placed with the applicant by an adoption agency or in pursuance of an order of the High Court; or

    (b)   for at least 12 months in any other case.

(17) (Paragraph 18) Notice does not have to be given if the child was placed with the applicant by an adoption agency. Where notice does have to be given, no order can be made until the expiration of three months from the date of the notice.

(18) (Paragraph 19) The nature of the proceedings and the date and effect of any orders made should be stated. The court cannot proceed with the application if a previous application made by the same applicant in relation to the child was refused, unless one of the conditions in section 24(1) of the Adoption Act 1976 is satisfied. The Court must dismiss the application if it considers that, where the application is made by a married couple of whom one is a parent and the other a step-parent of the child or by a step-parent of the child alone, the matter would be better dealt with under Part 1 of the Children Act 1989.

(19) (Paragraph 21) Enter the name and address of the adoption agency or individual who took part in the arrangements for placing the child for adoption in the home of the applicant.

(20) (Paragraph 22) Where the applicant or one of the applicants is a parent of the child, or a relative as defined by section 72(1) of the Adoption Act 1976 or the child was placed with the applicants by an adoption agency, no referee need be named.

(21) (Paragraph 23) If the applicant wishes his identity to be kept confidential, the serial number obtained under rule 14 should be given.

F2. Agreement to Adoption Order

[Heading as F1]

If you are in any doubt about your legal rights you should obtain legal advice before signing this form

Whereas an application is to be/has been made [by .... and .... *or* under serial number ....] (1)

for an adoption order or an order authorising a proposed foreign adoption in respect of (2) a child, and whereas the child is the person to whom the birth certificate attached marked "A" relates; (3)

[and whereas the child is at least six weeks old].
I, the undersigned ....
of ....
being a parent/guardian (4) of the child hereby state as follows:

1. I understand that the effect of an adoption order/an order authorising a proposed foreign adoption will be to deprive me permanently of parental responsibility for the child and to vest it in the applicant(s); and in particular I understand that, if an order is made, I shall have no right to see or get in touch with the child or to have him/her returned to me.

2. I further understand that the court cannot make an adoption order/ an order authorising the proposed foreign adoption of the child without the agreement of each parent or guardian of the child unless the court dispenses with an agreement on the ground that the person concerned:

(a) cannot be found or is incapable of giving agreement, or
(b) is withholding his/her agreement unreasonably, or
(c) has persistently failed without reasonable cause to discharge the parental responsibility for the child, or
(d) has abandoned or neglected the child, or
(e) has persistently ill-treated the child, or
(f) has seriously ill-treated the child and the rehabilitation of the child within the household of the parent or guardian is unlikely.

3. I further understand that when the application for an adoption order/order authorising the proposed foreign adoption of the child is heard, this document may be used as evidence of my agreement to the making of the order unless I inform the court that I no longer agree. (5)

4. I hereby freely, and with full understanding of what is involved, agree unconditionally to the making of an adoption order/an order authorising the proposed foreign adoption of the child in pursuance of the application.

5. As far as I know, the only person(s) or body(ies) who has/have taken part in the arrangements for the child's adoption is/are [and ....] (6)

6. I have not received or given any payment or reward for, or in consideration of the adoption of the child, for any agreement to the making of an adoption order or placing the child for adoption with any person or making any arrangements for the adoption of the child [other than a payment to an adoption agency for their expenses incurred in connection with the adoption].

IF YOU ARE IN ANY DOUBT ABOUT YOUR LEGAL RIGHTS YOU SHOULD OBTAIN LEGAL ADVICE BEFORE SIGNING THIS FORM

Signature ....
This form, duly completed, was signed by ....
the said ....
before me at ....
on the .... day of ....
Signature ....
Address ....
Description ....(7)

NOTES

(1) Insert either the name(s) of the applicant(s) or the serial number assigned to the applicant(s) for the purposes of the application.

(2) Insert the first name(s) and surname of the child as known to the person giving the agreement.

(3) If the child has previously been adopted a certified copy of the entry in the Adopted Childrens Register should be attached and not a certified copy of the original entry in the Register of Births. Where two or more forms of agreement are supplied to the court at the same time they may both or all refer to a certificate attached to one of the forms of agreement.

(4) The father of a child who was not married to the child's mother when the child was born is not a parent for this purpose unless he has parental responsibility by virtue of a court order or an agreement or he has a residence order in respect of the child; "guardian" also means a person appointed by deed or will in accordance with the provisions of the Guardianship of Infants Acts 1886 and 1925 or the Guardianship of Minors Act 1971 or the Children Act 1989, or by a court of competent jurisdiction or under section 5 of the Children Act 1989 to be the guardian of the child.

(5) Notice will be given of the hearing of the application and of the court by which it is to be heard. After the making of the application a parent or guardian who has agreed cannot remove the child from the home of the applicant(s) except with leave of the court.

(6) Enter the name and address of the adoption agency or individual who took part in the arrangements for placing the child in the actual custody of the applicant(s).

(7) In England and Wales this form should be witnessed by the reporting officer. In Scotland, it should be witnessed by a Justice of the Peace or a Sheriff and in Northern Ireland, by a Justice of the Peace. Outside the United Kingdom it should be witnessed by a person authorised by law in the place where the document is signed to administer an oath for any judicial or legal purpose, a British consular officer, a notary public, or, if the person executing the document is serving in the regular armed forces of the Crown, an officer holding a commission in any of those forces.

F3. Notice of Hearing

[Heading as F1]

To *name*
of *address*

Whereas an application for [an adoption order *or* an order authorising a proposed foreign adoption] in respect of *name* a child of the male/female sex born on the   day of   has been made

[by ....
and ....
of ....
or under the serial number ....][(1)]

[and whereas ....
was/were appointed reporting officer(s)]
[and whereas ....
was appointed guardian ad litem of the child];

Take notice

[1. The said application will be heard[(2)] before the Judge at [the Royal Courts of Justice, Strand, London WC2A 2LL] on the   day of .... at .... o'clock

and that you may then appear and be heard on the question whether an adoption order/order authorising a proposed foreign adoption should be made]

[2. That if you wish to appear and be heard on the question whether an adoption order/order authorising a proposed foreign adoption should be made, you should give notice to the court on or before the   day of   in order that a time may be fixed for your appearance][(3)]

3. That you are not obliged to attend the hearing unless you wish to do so or the court notifies you that your attendance is necessary.

4. That while the application is pending a parent or guardian of the child who has agreed to the making of an order must not, except with the leave of the court, remove the child from the home of the applicant.

[5. That the application states that the child has had his/her home with the applicant for the five years preceding the application and accordingly, if that is correct, no person is entitled, against the will of the applicant, to remove the child from the applicant's home except with the leave of the court or under authority conferred by an enactment or on the arrest of the child](4)

[6. That the court has been requested to dispense with your agreement to the making of an order on the ground(s) that(5):

....
....
....

and a statement of facts on which the applicant intends to rely is attached]

IT WOULD ASSIST THE COURT IF YOU WOULD COMPLETE THE ATTACHED FORM AND RETURN IT TO ME

Dated the .... day of ....

Signature
District Judge

To the [Senior District Judge of the Family Division *or* District Judge of the .... County Court
Number .... of ....

I received notice of the hearing of the application on the .... day of ....
I [do not] wish to oppose the application
I [do not] wish to appear and be heard on the question whether an order should be made

Signature
Address
Date

NOTES

(1) Enter the name of the applicant(s) unless the applicant has obtained a serial number, in which case the second part in brackets should be completed.

(2) When this form is used under rule 25(2) of the Adoption Rules 1984 to give notice of a further hearing of an application it is to be amended so as to refer to a further hearing and so as to give particulars of the interim order.

(3) (Paragraphs 1 and 2) Paragraph 1 should be completed and paragraph 2 struck out where the notice is addressed to any respondent where the applicant does not wish his identity to be kept confidential. When a serial number has been assigned to the applicant and the notice is addressed to an individual respondent other than the spouse of the applicant, paragraph 1 should be struck out and paragraph 2 completed

(4) This paragraph should be deleted except where it appears from the originating process that the child has had his/her home with the applicant for five years

(5) Unless deleted this paragraph should contain the grounds specified in the originating application

F4. Notice of Intention to Apply to Dispense with Agreement

[Heading as F1]

TAKE NOTICE that the Applicant intends to apply to dispense with your agreement to the making of an adoption order herein

A copy of the statement of facts on which the applicant(s) intends to rely is sent herewith

Dated the .... day of ....

Signature
District Judge

F5. Statement of Facts

[Heading as in F1]

1. The child *name* was born on the .... day of .... Her mother *name* was not married. She lived with the father of the child *name* for approximately six months. They were students in their first year at University.

2. The mother and father entered into a parental responsibility agreement on the .... day of .... the day after the said child was born. They separated two weeks after the birth of the said child.

3. On the .... day of .... the child was placed with the Applicants as long term foster parents with a view to adoption. She has settled in well and become an integrated member of the family which comprises the Applicants and their natural son who is eight years of age. Neither the mother nor the father has had contact with the child since she was placed with the Applicants.

4. The mother consents to the application but the father has failed to give his consent. The ground on which the Applicants will ask the court to dispense with the consent of the father is that *e.g. he cannot be found. He left University when he left the mother of the child and has not had any contact with her since. Extensive enquiries have been made but no trace can be found. He did talk to the mother of going to Africa and it may be that he has gone to live there.*

(Signature)

F6. Interim Order for Adoption

[Heading as F1]
Before [Mr. Justice *or* His Honour Judge] .... in Chambers
In the matter of the Adoption Act 1976
In the matter of *name* a child

WHEREAS an application has been made by *(name of applicant)* of *(address)* [and *(name)*] for an adoption order in respect of *(name)* a child of the male/female sex, the child/adopted child of *(name)* [and *(name)*];

IT IS ORDERED [that the determination of the application be postponed and that the applicant(s) do have parental responsibility for the child until the .... day of .... by way of a probationary period *or* that the determination of the application be postponed to the .... day of ...., and that the applicant(s) do have parental responsibility for the child until that day by way of a probationary period]

[upon the following terms, namely *(state them)*];
[and as regards costs IT IS ORDERED that *(give order for costs)*;]

[AND IT IS ORDERED that the application be further heard before the judge on the ....

day of .... at .... o'clock

DATED the .... day of ....

F7. Abridged Adoption Order

[Heading as F6]

UPON HEARING [Counsel *or* the Solicitors] for the Applicants and the Respondents

AND UPON READING *(recite evidence)*

IT IS ORDERED that the Applicant(s) do adopt the child

AND the Judge further orders that the costs of the said child of incidental to and in connection with this application be taxed on the standard basis and that the applicant(s) do pay to the said child such costs as taxed

AND IT IS RECORDED that the .... Council was notified of the applicant(s) intention to apply for an adoption order in respect of the child and that the ....

took part in the arrangements for placing the child in the actual custody of the applicant(s) with a view to adoption

AND IT IS DIRECTED that the Registrar General shall make an entry in the Adopted Children Register

DATED the ....day of ....

Appendix to Order

[Heading as F1]

In the Matter of the Adoption Act 1976
And in the Matter of the Children Act 1989
And in the Matter of *name* a child

This appendix forms part of the adoption order but shall not form part of any copy supplied to any person other than the Registrar General

1. The agreement of *(name)* of *(address)* the [parent or guardian] of the child is dispensed with on the ground(s) that[1] *state grounds*

[2. The order is made on the application of one person who [is married *or is* the [father or mother] of the child] and the court is satisfied that[2] *state appropriate grounds*]

NOTES

(1) Enter the appropriate grounds in section 16(2) of the Adoption Act 1976
(2) Enter the appropriate grounds in section 15(1)(b) or (3) of the Adoption Act 1976, and specify where appropriate the matters on which the court is satisfied.

G. Application for Financial Provision

THE LAW

3–33 Paragraph 1 of Schedule 1 to the Children Act 1989 enables the court to make a maintenance order, a settlement or transfer of property order in favour of a child against either or both of its parents. Paragraph 2 enables the court to make a periodical payments order and lump sum order in favour of a child who has reached 18 if that child is or will be receiving instruction at an educational establishment or undergoing training for a trade profession or vocation or there are special circumstances justifying the making of an order. Again the order can be made against either or both parents so long as the parents are not living together. An application cannot be made if immediately before the child reached the age of 16 a periodical payments order was already in force.

Paragraph 10 enables the court to alter any written agreement made by the parents of a child which contains provisions in respect of the making or securing of payments or the disposition or use of any property for the maintenance or education of the child. The court may vary or revoke any of the financial arrangements as may appear just if satisfied that there has been a change in the circumstances warranting the alteration of the arrangements or that the agreement does not contain proper financial arrangements for the child. The variation can take place either during the lifetime of the parent or after the death of one of them.[11]

3–34 The Child Support Act 1991 limits the court's jurisdiction to order child maintenance or to vary agreements for maintenance to cases where:

(a) one or more of the absent parents, the person with care or the child in question is not habitually resident in the U.K.;
(b) the child is married, over 19 or over 16 and not in advanced education;
(c) the parties seek a consent order in the terms of a written agreement;
(d) a top up order is sought;
(e) a school fees order is sought;
(f) expenses for a disabled child are sought;
(g) the claim is against a person with care.

---

[11] Para. 11.

The Procedure

Court

3–35 The High Court and county court have equal jurisdiction. The family proceedings court can only award lump sums up to £1,000 and cannot order the transfer or settlement of property or secured periodical payments.

Pleadings

3–36 Application is made on Forms C1 and C10 explaining the grounds for the application, with a statement of means in Form C10A. The respondent, *i.e.* any parent who is not an applicant and any person whom the applicant believes to be interested in or affected by the proceedings, must file Form C9 within 14 days of service.

Service

3–37 The applicant must lodge one set of forms for the court and one for each respondent. The court provides Form C6 (notice to parties) and Form C6A (notice to non-parties) endorsed with the date of hearing, and C7 (acknowledgment) and the applicant must serve these at least 14 days before the hearing or directions appointment. At the first appointment, the applicant must file a statement of service in Form C9.

Directions

3–38 The court can give directions timetabling and ordering the filing of written statements, including the filing of a statement of means in Form C10A by the respondent, and such other directions as it thinks fit. The court can also make an interim order for periodical payments.

Order

3–39 On an application for a child under 18, the court can order periodical payments, secured periodical payments, lump sum and/or settlement or transfer of property.

On an application by a child over 18, the court can order periodical payments or a lump sum.

On an application to alter a maintenance agreement, the court can vary or revoke any financial arrangements and can insert provision for periodical payments or for security for increasing or decreasing the level of periodical payments.

The Precedents

> Form C1 .... Appendix, p. 158.
> Form C2 .... Appendix, p. 163.
> Form C6 .... Appendix, p. 165.
> Form C6A .... Appendix, p. 167.
> Form C7 .... Appendix, p. 169.
> Form C9 .... Appendix, p. 171.
> Form C10 .... Appendix, p. 172.
> Form C10A .... Appendix, p. 175.

Part IV: Actions for Protection from Domestic Violence

A. Applications under Part IV of the Family Law Act 1996

The Law

The Family Law Act repeals the whole of the Domestic Violence and Matrimonial Proceedings Act 1976 with effect from October 1, 1997 but does not prevent an existing order from remaining in force or affect the enforcement of an existing order.[1] A broader group, including people living in single sex relationships, ex-spouses, friends and relatives, may apply for a non-molestation order but may only apply for an occupation order if the applicant is entitled to occupy because of a beneficial interest or contract or statute. Otherwise the legislation is still limited to cohabitants who live or have lived together as husband and wife. As this book is about the legal remedies available to cohabitants, it does not go into the provisions of Part IV of the FLA dealing with spouses.

4–01

Non-molestation orders[2]

An order prohibiting the respondent from molesting a person with whom he or she is associated or a relevant child, may be made on the application of the associated person or in any family proceedings where the court considers the order should be made for the benefit of any other party or any relevant child.

4–02

The court must take into account all the circumstances including the need to secure the health, safety and wellbeing of the applicant and any relevant child.

---

[1] Sched. 10 and para. 10, Sched. 9.
[2] FLA, s. 42.

Occupation orders

4–03 An occupation order can be made in favour of an associated person entitled to occupy a house,[3] or in favour of a cohabitant or former cohabitant if they live or have lived as husband and wife whether entitled or not.[4]

Section 33 of the FLA—Applicant has an interest

4–04 If a person is entitled to occupy a house because of a beneficial interest or contract or statute giving him/her the right of occupation and the house is or has been or at any time was intended to be the home of the person entitled and another person with whom he or she is associated, then the person entitled may apply for an order:

(a) enforcing the applicant's entitlement to remain in occupation as against the respondent;
(b) requiring the respondent to allow the applicant to enter and remain;
(c) regulating the occupation of the house by either or both;
(d) if the respondent is "entitled"—prohibiting, suspending or restricting the exercise by him/her of his/her rights to occupy;
(e) [*refers to spouses*];
(f) requiring the respondent to leave the house or part;
(g) excluding the respondent from a defined area in which the house is included.

If the application is made by a formerly engaged person, it must be made within three years of termination of the agreement.[5]

The court shall take into account all the circumstances including:

(a) the housing needs and resources of each party and any relevant child;
(b) the financial resources of each party;
(c) the likely effect of any order or lack of order on the health, safety and well being of the parties and any relevant child;
(d) the conduct of the parties in relation to each other and otherwise.[6]

If it appears to the court that the applicant or a relevant child is likely to suffer significant harm attributable to the conduct of the

[3] s. 33.
[4] ss. 36, 38.
[5] s. 33(2).
[6] s. 33(6).

respondent if an order is not made, the court shall make the order unless it appears that the respondent or any relevant child is likely to suffer as great or greater significant harm if the order is made.[7]

Section 62(3)—Association

A person is associated with another if: 4–05

   (a) they are or have been married to each other;
   (b) they are cohabitants or former cohabitants. Cohabitants are defined as a man and a woman who, although not married to each other, are living together as husband and wife;
   (c) they live or have lived in the same household, otherwise than merely by reason of one of them being the other's employee, tenant, lodger or boarder;
   (d) they are relatives (defined in s. 63);
   (e) they have agreed to marry one another (whether or not that agreement has been terminated);
   (f) they are both parents of a child or have parental responsibility;
   (g) they are parties to the same family proceedings; or,
      in the case of adopted children or children freed for adoption,[8] one is the natural parent or natural grandparent and the other is the child or adoptive parent, adoption applicant or person with whom the child has at any time been placed for adoption.

Section 36—Applicant with no right to occupy

If one cohabitant or former cohabitant is "entitled" and the other is not, and the dwelling house is the home in which they live, have lived or intended to live together as husband and wife, the cohabitant or former cohabitant not so entitled may apply for an order: 4–06

   (i) if in occupation, giving the right not to be evicted or excluded from the house or any part of it for the period specified in the order and prohibiting the respondent from evicting or excluding during that period[9];
   (ii) if not in occupation, giving the right to enter and occupy the house for the period specified in the order and requiring the respondent to permit the exercise of that right.[10]

---

[7] s. 33(7) (balance of harm test).
[8] s. 62(5).
[9] s. 36(3).
[10] s. 36(4).

Section s.36(6). When deciding whether to make an order under section 36(3) or (4) the court shall consider all the circumstances including section 33(6)(a) to (d) *and:*

    (e) the nature of the parties' relationship—see section 41 below;
    (f) the length of time during which they have lived together as husband and wife;
    (g) whether there are or have been children of the relationship or for whom both parties have or have had parental responsibility;
    (h) the length of time elapsed since the parties ceased to live together;
    (i) whether there are any pending proceedings for orders for financial relief under the Children Act 1989 or relating to the legal or beneficial ownership of the house.

Section 36(5). An order may also:

    (a) regulate the occupation of the house by either or both;
    (b) prohibit, suspend or restrict the exercise by the respondent of the right to occupy;
    (c) require the respondent to leave the house or part of it;
    (d) exclude the respondent from a defined area in which the house is included.

Section 36(7). When deciding whether to make an order under section 36(5) the court shall consider all the circumstances including section 33(6)(a) to (d) and the balance of harm test. There is no duty to make an order if the balance of harm test is satisfied as there is under section 33(7).

Section 36(11). A person who has an equitable interest but not a legal estate in the house, is to be treated as not being entitled to occupy the house by virtue of that interest, but this section does not prejudice the right of such a person to apply for a section 33 order.

Section 38—Neither cohabitant entitled to occupy

4–07 If both cohabitants or former cohabitants occupy a house which is the home in which they live or lived together as husband and wife and neither is "entitled", either may apply for an order against the other:

    (a) requiring the respondent to allow the applicant to enter and remain in the house or part;
    (b) regulating the occupation of the house by either or both;

(c) requiring the respondent to leave the house or part or;
(d) excluding the respondent from a defined area in which the house is included.

Section 38(4). The court shall have regard to all the circumstances including section 33(6)(a) to (d) and the balance of harm test.

If in doubt about the appropriate form of relief, refer to the flowchart in Appendix 3.

Section 39—

An application for an occupation order may be made in other family proceedings or without other family proceedings being instituted and if an application is made under one section, the court can make an occupation order under another section if more appropriate. The fact that a person has applied for or been granted an occupation order, does not affect his/her right to claim a legal or equitable interest in property in any subsequent proceeding. **4–08**

Section 41—

Where the court is required to consider the nature of the parties' relationship, it is to have regard to the fact that they have not given each other the commitment involved in marriage. **4–09**

Section 43—Applications by children

A child under 16 may not apply for an occupation order or a non-molestation order except with the leave of the court and leave will only be granted if the court is satisfied that the child has sufficient understanding to make the application **4–10**

Section 44—Applications by engaged people

Applications by engaged or formerly engaged people must be supported by written evidence of agreement to marry or evidence of the gift of an engagement ring in contemplation of marriage or of a ceremony entered into by the parties witnessed by one or more persons. **4–11**

Section 45—Ex parte orders

The court may, in any case where it considers that it is just and convenient to do so, make an ex parte occupation order or non-molestation order. **4–12**

The court shall have regard to all the circumstances including:

(a) any risk of significant harm to the applicant or a relevant child, attributable to the conduct of the respondent, if the order is not made immediately;

(b) whether it is likely that the applicant will be deterred or prevented from pursuing the application if an order is not made immediately;
(c) whether there is reason to believe that the respondent is aware of the proceedings but is deliberately evading service and that the applicant or relevant child will be seriously prejudiced by the delay involved—
  (i) in magistrates court, in effecting service;
  (ii) in any other case, in effecting substituted service.

The court must then afford the respondent the opportunity to make representations as soon as just and convenient at a full hearing.

If an occupation order is made at a full hearing, the maximum period for the order will be taken as having started on the date the initial *ex parte* order first had effect and any extensions apply as if the full order and initial order were a single order.

Section 46—Undertakings

4-13 The court may accept an undertaking and this is enforceable as if it were an order of the court. No power of arrest may be attached to an undertaking and *the court shall not accept an undertaking in any case where a power of arrest would be attached to the order.*[11]

Section 47—Power of arrest

4-14 *Section 47(1) and (2).* If the court makes an occupation order or a non-molestation order and it appears that the respondent has used or threatened violence against the applicant or a relevant child, it *shall* attach a power of arrest unless satisfied in all the circumstances that the applicant or child will be adequately protected without it.

4-15 *Section 47(3).* The court may attach a power of arrest to an *ex parte* order if it appears that the respondent has used or threatened violence against the applicant or a relevant child and that there is a risk of significant harm to the applicant or child attributable to conduct of the respondent if a power of arrest is not attached immediately.

4-16 *Section 47(4) and (5).* The power of arrest may be for a shorter period than the main order and any such period may be extended on one or more occasions on an application to vary or discharge the order.

[11] s. 46(3).

Section 47(6) and (7). A constable may then arrest a person whom he has reasonable cause for suspecting to be in breach. If arrested, the respondent must be brought before the relevant judicial authority within 24 hours and if the matter is not disposed of, he or she may be remanded or the proceedings may be adjourned for up to 14 days, with not less than two business days' notice of the adjourned hearing. No account is taken of Christmas Day, Good Friday or any Sunday.

4–17

Section 47(8). If there is no power of arrest but the applicant considers that the respondent has failed to comply with the order, he or she may apply to the relevant judicial authority for the issue of a warrant for the respondent's arrest. Such an application must be substantiated on oath and the relevant judicial authority must have reasonable grounds for believing the respondent has failed to comply with the order before a warrant will be issued. If the matter is not disposed of when the respondent is brought before the court, he or she may be remanded in Form FL409—see section 47(10), section 48 and Schedule 5. The case may be adjourned for up to 14 days with not less than two business days' notice of the adjourned hearing. Committal procedures will follow the provisions of the CCR 1981, Ord. 29, r. 1 using Forms N78, N79, N80, N83 and N117 in the county court and new Forms FL418, FL419, FL420, FL421 and FL422. The court may adjourn consideration of the penalty to be imposed when a contempt is found proved, and may restore the matter if the respondent does not comply with any conditions specified.[12] It may also suspend execution of the committal order.

4–18

Applications for bail are dealt with in rule 3.10 of the Family Proceedings (Amendment No.3) Rules 1997.

Section 49. An occupation order or non-molestation order may be varied or discharged by the court on an application by the respondent or applicant and a non-molestation order and/or power of arrest may be varied or discharged by the court even though no such application has been made.

4–19

Section 53—Transfer of tenancies

Part I of Schedule 7 provides that if one cohabitant is entitled, in his/her own right or jointly with the other cohabitant, to occupy a house in which they lived together as husband and wife by virtue of a relevant tenancy, and the cohabitants cease to live together, the court can make a Part II order. The court shall have regard to all the circumstances including:

4–20

---

[12] Rule 3.9A(6) of the Family Proceedings (Amendment No. 3) Rules 1997.

(a) the circumstances in which the tenancy was granted;
(b) the matters mentioned in section 33(6)(a) to (c) and section 36(6)(e) to (h); and
(c) the suitability of the parties as tenants

Part II orders:

4–21 *Protected, secure or assured tenancy or assured agricultural occupancy.* If the tenancy was a protected tenancy under the Rent Act 1977, a secure tenancy under the Housing Act 1985 or an assured tenancy or assured agricultural occupancy under Part I of the Housing Act 1988, the court may order that with effect from a date specified in the order the interest of one cohabitant be transferred and vested in the other cohabitant

4–22 *Statutory tenancy within the meaning of the Rent Act 1977 or the Rent (Agriculture) Act 1976.* The court may order that with effect from a date specified in the order, one cohabitant is to cease to be entitled to occupy and the other cohabitant is to be deemed to be the tenant.

Part III of Schedule 7 provides that the court may order the cohabitant to whom the tenancy was transferred to pay compensation to the other cohabitant. Payment can be deferred until a specific date or event or paid by instalments if immediate payment would cause the transferee financial hardship. The court shall have regard to all the circumstances including:

(a) the financial loss that would otherwise be suffered by the transferor as a result of the order;
(b) the financial needs and resources of the parties; and
(c) the financial obligations of the parties.

If the court makes a Part II order, it may direct that both cohabitants are to be jointly and severally liable to discharge any or all of the liabilities and obligations in respect of the house which have fallen due before the date of transfer and may direct either cohabitant to indemnify the other.

The landlord will be given the opportunity of being heard.

Transitional provisions

4–23 Nothing in Part IV of the FLA prevents an existing order from remaining in force or affects the enforcement of an existing order.[13] As orders existing at the time Part IV came into force should be limited in time, this provision will be of dwindling significance.

---

[13] Sched. 9, para. 10.

Nothing affects any application to extend, vary or discharge an existing order, but the court may treat the application as an application for a Part IV order, if it thinks it just and reasonable to do so. The making of a Part IV order between parties about whom an existing order is in force, discharges the existing order.

Protection of children

Part IV of the FLA amends the Children Act so that, whereas before it was necessary to remove the child from the home on the making of an emergency protection order, it is now possible to obtain an order excluding the person suspected of causing the child to suffer significant harm. This book does not deal with public law in general but Schedule 6 to the FLA inserts a new section 44A of the Children Act 1989 so that if the court is satisfied that an emergency protection order should be made and that there is reasonable cause to believe that if a person is excluded from the house in which the child lives, the child will not be likely to suffer significant harm or that inquiries will not be frustrated, and that another person living in the house is able and willing to care for the child and consents to the exclusion requirement, an exclusion requirement may be included in the emergency protection order. Such an exclusion requirement may require the person to leave the house, prohibit the person from entering the house and may exclude the person from a defined area in which the house is situated. A power of arrest may be attached. The court may accept an undertaking from the relevant person. 4–24

THE PROCEDURE

The rules are contained in the Family Proceedings (Amendment No.3) Rules 1997,[14] the Family Proceedings Courts (Matrimonial Proceedings, etc.) (Amendment) Rules 1997[15] and the Family Proceedings Courts (Children Act 1989)(Amendment) Rules 1997.[16] 4–25

Court

The court means any court with family jurisdiction and applications will generally be made to a divorce county court, family hearing centre or care centre or a family proceedings court. Applications to the High Court will be allowed if there are pending family 4–26

---

[14] S.I. 1997 No. 1893 (L. 29).
[15] S.I. 1997 No. 1894 (L. 30).
[16] S.I. 1997 No. 1895 (L. 31).

proceedings there. Free standing applications by children under 16 for leave to apply must be made to the High Court but then if leave is granted, the High Court can either hear the matter itself or remit it for hearing in the county court. If the child applies in existing proceedings in the lower courts, the application for leave only should be transferred to the High Court. It is possible to transfer up, down or sideways on specific grounds. Proceedings must be transferred from a family proceedings court to a county court where a child under 18 is the respondent or wishes to become a party and where a party is a person who by reason of a mental disorder within the meaning of the Mental Health Act 1983 is incapable of managing and administering his or her affairs. Proceedings may be transferred if there is a conflict with the law of another jurisdiction, a novel and difficult point of law, a question of general public interest or the proceedings are exceptionally complex.

There is a general power to transfer between county courts where the court considers it necessary or expedient and where there is a dispute about a person's entitlement to occupy[17] the case may be transferred if the property is in the district of another court. A magistrates' court will not be competent to entertain any application, or make any order, involving any disputed question as to a party's entitlement to occupy any property by virtue of a beneficial interest or estate or contract or statute giving him or her the right to remain in occupation, unless it is unnecessary to determine the question in order to deal with the application or make the order. A magistrates' court may decline jurisdiction in any proceedings if it considers that the case can more conveniently be dealt with by another court.[18] It cannot deal with applications to transfer of tenancy.

Pleadings

4–27 Proceedings are begun using a single prescribed form, Form FL401, no matter which court or which type of order is being sought. An application by a child under 16 is made on the same form but is treated initially as an application for leave. Solicitors may produce their own version of the forms provided they first obtain permission of the Stationery Office[19], the content of their version is the same as the prescribed form and the format is not substantially different.

If the applicant is concerned about giving their address, they can complete Confidential Address Form C8. If they do not know all

---

[17] s. 59(1).
[18] s. 59.
[19] Stationery Office, Copyright Unit, Clements House, 2–16 Colegate, Norwich NR3 1BQ.

the details requested on the form, they should say so where appropriate.

The application must be supported by a statement (sworn to be true for the county court and declared to be true for the family proceedings court) setting out the reasons for applying for the order giving as much detail with dates as possible. In the family proceedings court, oral evidence may be acceptable with the leave of the court.

If applying for an *ex parte* order, it should deal with the matters referred to in section 45 mentioned above, *i.e.* risk of significant harm if an order is not made immediately, whether the applicant would be prevented or deterred from proceeding if an order is not made immediately, and whether the respondent is deliberately evading service and the applicant would be prejudiced by the delay.

If applying for an occupation order, it should deal with the matters referred to in section 33(6)(a) to (d), *i.e.* the respective housing needs and resources of the parties and any relevant child, the financial resources of each of the parties, the likely effect of any order or lack of order on the health, safety and wellbeing of the parties or any relevant child, the conduct of the parties to each other, and also the balance of harm test.

If the cohabitant respondent is the sole legal owner or tenant, it should deal with the matters referred to in section 36 (6)(e) to (i), *i.e.* describe the nature of the relationship, bearing in mind section 41, how long the parties lived together, whether there were any children, how long since they stopped living together and whether there are any pending proceedings under Schedule I to the Children Act or relating to the property.

If the applicant is applying on the basis that he or she had agreed to marry the respondent, it should deal with section 33(2) and say when the agreement came to an end and deal with section 44 and say what evidence there is of the agreement to marry.

The respondent may file a statement, sworn for county court or declared to be true for family proceedings court, in response.

An application for a transfer of tenancy under section 53 and Schedule 7, must be made by originating application with an affidavit in support setting out the circumstances in which the tenancy was granted and the suitability of the parties as tenants as well as the matters under section 33 (6)(a) to (c) and section 36(6)(e) to (h). Such applications are governed by the rules relating to applications under section 17 of the Married Women's Property Act 1882 (F.P.R. 1991 r.36(7) to (9). See Part I, Section C.

An application for an exclusion requirement to be inserted in an emergency protection order must be made on the supplement for an application for an Emergency Protection Order C11 and the applicant must prepare a separate statement of the evidence in

4–28

support of that requirement. The consent of the person caring for the child may be given orally to the court or in writing and if in writing, it must say that the person giving consent is able and willing to give the child the care which it would be reasonable to expect a parent to give and understands that the giving of the consent could lead to the exclusion of the relevant person from the house in which the child lives.

Service

4–29 The application must be served personally on the respondent not less than two business days before the hearing. There is power to abridge time for service and the court can make an order for substituted service. Responsibility for service rests with the parties rather than the court. If the applicant is acting in person, he or she can ask the court to effect service. If personal service is not practicable, service can be effected in accordance with rule 10.2 or 10.3 of the Family Proceedings Rules 1991, *i.e.* by first class post, document exchange, fax or leaving the document at the respondent's address or solicitor's address. The application must be served with the statement in support and Notice of Proceedings Form FL402 giving the respondent notice of the hearing date. A statement of service must be filed.

A copy of any application for an occupation order or transfer of tenancy order must be served by first class post on the mortgagee or landlord with a notice in Form FL416 informing him of his right to make representations at or before the hearing of the application in the presence of both parties.

Where there is an application for an exclusion requirement to be inserted in an emergency protection order, the separate statement in support must be served personally on the relevant person and the relevant person should be informed of his right to apply to vary or discharge the exclusion requirement.

Directions

4–30 The court can give, vary or rescind directions for the conduct of the proceedings dealing with matters such as service, time tabling and evidence.

On applications for a transfer of tenancy, the court has the same powers of giving directions as in an application for ancillary relief *e.g.* discovery, further particulars, etc.

Order

4–31 Under section 33, an order may:

(a) enforce the applicant's entitlement to remain in occupation as against the respondent;
(b) require the respondent to permit the applicant to enter and remain in the dwelling-house or part of it;
(c) regulate the occupation of the dwelling-house by either or both of the parties;
(d) prohibit, suspend or restrict the exercise of any right to occupy which the respondent may have;
(e) require the respondent to leave the dwelling-house or part of it; or
(f) exclude the respondent from a defined area in which the dwelling-house is included.

An order under this section may declare that the applicant is entitled to occupy the dwelling-house by virtue of a beneficial estate or interest or contract or by virtue of any enactment giving him or her the right to remain in occupation. The order may be made for a specified period, until the occurrence of a specified event or until further order.

Under section 36, if the applicant is in occupation, an order must:

(a) give the applicant the right not to be evicted or excluded from the dwelling-house or any part of it by the respondent for the period specified in the order; and
(b) prohibit the respondent from evicting or excluding the applicant during that period.

If the applicant is not in occupation, an order must:

(a) give the applicant the right to enter into and occupy the dwelling-house for the period specified in the order; and
(b) require the respondent to permit the exercise of that right.

An order under this section may also provide as stated under section 33(6)(c) to (f) above. Any order under this section must be limited so as to have effect for a specified period not exceeding six months, but may be extended on one occasion for a further specified period not exceeding six months.

Under section 38, an order may provide as stated under section 33(6)(b)(c)(e) and (f) above. An order under this section must be limited in time in the same way as a section 36 order.

Section 40. On or after making an occupation order, the court may: **4–32**

(a) impose on either party obligations as to repair and maintenance of the house or the discharge of rent, mortgage or other outgoings;

(b) order a party occupying the house to make periodical payments to the other if the other would, but for the order, be "entitled" to occupy;
(c) grant either party possession or use of furniture or other contents;
(d) order either party to take reasonable care of any furniture or other contents;
(e) order either party to take reasonable steps to keep the house and any furniture or other contents secure.

The court shall have regard to all the circumstances including financial needs and resources and financial obligations. Such an order ceases to have effect when the occupation order ceases to have effect.

Under section 42, an order may prohibit the respondent from molesting the applicant and/or a relevant child. The order may refer to molestation in general, to particular acts of molestation or both. The order may be for a specified period or until further order. An order made in other family proceedings ceases to have affect if those proceedings are withdrawn or dismissed.

The court may attach a penal notice to an occupation order but must attach a penal notice to an order including both non-molestation and occupation provisions.

An emergency protection order or interim care order including an exclusion requirement will be made in Forms C23 or C33. If the applicant removes the child from the house for a continuous period of more than 24 hours, the exclusion requirement ceases to have effect.

Enforcement

4–33 Where a power of arrest is attached to one or more provisions of an order, those provisions will be set out in Form FL406. This form should be delivered to the officer for the time being in charge of the police station for the applicant's address or such other station as the court specifies. Delivery is normally the responsibility of the applicant. It must be accompanied by a statement showing that the respondent has been served with the order or informed of its terms (because he was present when the order was made or by telephone or otherwise).

An application for a warrant of arrest must be made on Form FL407 and the warrant is in Form FL408. In the county court the warrant is executed by the bailiffs and in the magistrates court it is delivered by the justices' clerk to the police station for the respondent's address or such other station as the court specifies.

The Precedents

A1. Application

> See Form FL401, Appendix, p. 188.

A2. Affidavit in Support

[High Court or county court heading as appropriate]

Applicant
[name]
1st
[date]

I *[name]* of *[address and occupation and description]* make oath and say as follows:

1. I am the Applicant herein and I make this affidavit in support of my application for an order restraining the Respondent from molesting me and requiring him to leave our home.

2. I met the Respondent in about August *[year]* and by January *[year]* he had moved into my flat at *[address]*. We have lived together at that address as husband and wife since then. The flat is rented from *[name]* Council and the tenancy is in my sole name. I have lived there with my daughter *[name and date of birth]* from a previous relationship since June *[year]*.

3. I also have a son *[name and date of birth]*. The Respondent is the father.

4. The Respondent has always had a quick temper and has lashed out at things and thrown things but his behaviour has deteriorated over the last six months since he was made redundant.

5. On numerous occasions the precise dates of which I cannot remember the Respondent has pushed me in the chest or slapped my face. On one occasion in January this year he became very short tempered during the evening because our son was crying a lot and he kept shouting at me to do something about it. I eventually got the baby settled and we went to bed. He then wanted to have sex but I was very tired and said I didn't feel like it. He went berserk, punching me in the face and body and pulling my hair. I curled up in a ball and eventually he stopped and left the room. I

was absolutely petrified and locked the bedroom door but he did not try to return that night. He slept on the sofa. I sustained a black eye and bruising to my neck, right arm and back. The next morning I asked him to leave and he left.

6. Three days later he telephoned to say how sorry he was, that it would never happen again and that he wanted to see the children. He came to see the children on a regular basis and after two weeks I agreed to let him move back in.

7. On the 23rd February he went out drinking with some friends and spent all of our benefits. I asked him how we were going to pay for food and nappies which we desperately needed and he totally lost control. He punched me hard on the side of the head and I fell to the floor. He then started kicking me whilst I lay on the floor. My daughter was frightened and was crying and tried to pull his leg to pull him off me. He shook her away and stomped upstairs. I grabbed the baby and my daughter and ran next door where my neighbour called the police. They eventually arrived but said there was nothing they could do unless I pressed charges against him. They said there was no evidence of assault and they could only arrest him if I got an injunction with a power of arrest attached.

8. I spent the night with my neighbour but I had to return home the next day as I had nowhere else to go and everything I needed was in there. The Respondent laughed at me and taunted me about how the police had not done anything.

9. That evening I was cooking chips for tea when he came into the kitchen and started taunting me again. I told him that I was frightened by what he had done and that I wanted him to leave. He said there was no way he was leaving again. He said that he had had to crawl back to me last time and there was no way he was doing that again. I said that in that case I would get an injunction to keep him away from me. He said that if I went anywhere near a solicitor or a court he would finish us all off and he didn't care if he did time for it. He held the chip knife up to my throat and asked me if I understood. I really believe he meant what he said and I was very frightened.

10. Three days later I told him that I would like to go to bingo with my neighbour and that I had arranged for my mother to look after the children. He said I couldn't go and started ranting and raving and slamming things about. I went to get changed and when I came back into the lounge he started pulling my clothes off me and pulled a chain from round my neck which really hurt. He then said that if I was going out he would make sure no-one wanted to look at me and he got a knife and lunged towards my face. I jumped out of the way and he chased me round the room waving

the knife about and on one occasion it caught my right arm. The front door bell then rang and I managed to get to the door before he did. It was my mother who had come to collect the children and I screamed to her to call the police. They came much more quickly this time and took him down to the police station because they could see the gash on my arm.

11. I stayed the night with my mother but I cannot stay there indefinitely because there is not enough room. I wish to live in my own flat with my children but I am frightened to return there whilst there is a possibility that the Respondent will return. He has been released on police bail with no conditions about not returning to my flat. If an order is not made excluding the Respondent from my flat, I fear that he will be violent towards me again. He could stay with his brother or go back to his parents. Requiring him to leave would not cause him to suffer as much harm as if no order was made and he was violent to me again.

SWORN at
in the County of
this   day of

BEFORE ME

A3. Statement of Service

> See Form FL415, Appendix, p. 210.

A4. Order

> See Form FL404, Appendix, p. 199.

A5. Application to Vary, Extend or Discharge

> See Form FL403, Appendix, p. 197.

A6. Power of Arrest

> See Form FL406, Appendix, p. 207.

A7. Application for Warrant of Arrest

> See Form FL407, Appendix, p. 208.

A8. Affidavit in support of application for Warrant of Arrest

[High Court or county court heading as appropriate]

Applicant
[name]
2nd
[date]

I *[name]* of *[address and occupation and description]* make oath and say as follows:

1. I am the Applicant herein and I make this affidavit in support of my application for a warrant for the arrest of the Respondent for breach of an order made by this Court on the *[date]*.

2. There is now produced and shown to me marked "*AB*1" a true copy of the said injunction order from which it can be seen that the Respondent was forbidden to use violence against me and was forbidden from approaching within 100 metres of *[address]*.

3. I am informed by my solicitor and believe that the Respondent was personally served with a copy of the said injunction order on the *[date]*. He did move out of the property on that day and I moved back in with my two children.

4. At 6 o'clock the next evening the *[date]* I received a telephone call from a neighbour to say that the Respondent was standing outside the block of flats looking up at my flat. I looked out of the window and saw him there. I looked out again an hour later and he was still there. I then called the police and they came and moved him on.

5. At about 10 a.m. the following day, the *[date]* the Respondent came to the door of my flat and rang the bell. I saw that it was him through the spy hole in the door and I ignored him. He then started banging on the door with his fists and shouting to me to open the door. I told him that I would not open the door and that I intended to call the police. He then left.

6. Later that afternoon, at about 3.30 p.m. I had to go out to get some shopping and as I came out of the main entrance to the block of flats, the Respondent suddenly appeared at my side. I refused to

speak to him and carried on walking but he turned and stood in front of me blocking my way. I tried to walk round him but he grabbed hold of my shirt with two hands and shook me. He brought his face right up close to mine and shouted at me to speak to him. I still said nothing and he put his hands round my throat and squeezed and shook me. Just then a man walking on the other side of the street shouted at him to stop and he loosened his grip. I managed to get away and I ran back inside the flats and into a neighbour's flat. I sustained bruising to my neck.

7. I am now petrified of leaving my flat in case the Respondent is around and is violent towards me again. He clearly does not intend to obey the injunction order and I ask this court to punish him by sending him to prison.

SWORN at

in the County of
this   day of

BEFORE ME

A9. Warrant of arrest

See Form FL408, Appendix, p. 209.

A10. Notice to Mortgagees and Landowners

See Form FL416, Appendix, p. 211.

A11. Transfer of Proceedings

See Form FL417, Appendix, p. 212.

A12. Supplement for an Application for an Emergency Protection Order

See Form C11, Appendix, p. 179.

A13. Emergency Protection Order

See Form C23, Appendix, p. 181.

A14. Interim Care Order

See Form C33, Appendix, p. 183.

B. Applications in tort

THE LAW

4–34 It seems unlikely that applications in tort will be necessary since the implementation of Part IV of the Family Law Act 1996 (FLA). They used to be made when applications under the Domestic Violence and Matrimonial Proceedings Act 1976 (DVMPA) were not appropriate, *e.g.* the cohabitants were of the same sex, friends or relations or where the parties had already separated at the time of the last incident of violence relied upon. In these cases it would be possible to obtain an injunction in tort if a tortious act had been or was likely to be committed, *i.e.* assault, trespass or nuisance. It was unlikely that an exclusion order would be made except in those cases where the applicant had a property interest in the home and the respondent did not and the applicant could establish that the respondent entered as trespasser. Under section 42 of the FLA non-molestation orders can be made to protect a much wider group than before and the definition of associated persons will include most people previously excluded by the DVMPA.

However, a person who has never lived with his or her girlfriend or boyfriend as husband and wife or in the same household might need protection. Similarly, there could be trouble between a former cohabitant and a new cohabitant. Such people might still avail themselves of protection in tort.

THE PROCEDURE

Court

4–35 Application can be made in the High Court or the county court for the district in which the defendant resides or the cause of action wholly or partly arose.

Pleadings

4–36 A summons with particulars of claim must be issued and the application for the injunction is made as an interlocutory application. No other remedy, such as damages, need be sought. A free-standing injunction can be granted. The application is in Form N16A (Appendix, p. 215) with an affidavit in support. An application can be made *ex parte* where the plaintiff is likely to suffer harm unless an injunction is granted before notice is given. The reasons must be given in the affidavit.

The defendant may, but is not required to, serve an affidavit in reply and/or make a cross-application.

Service

The application and affidavit must be served at least two working days before the hearing unless the court had abridged time for service.

4–37

Order

The order is issued in Form N16 (Appendix, p. 213) forbidding any tort already committed or threatened. If an ex parte order is made, a date is given for further consideration. The injunction must be personally served.

4–38

The Precedents

B1. Particulars of claim

IN THE   COUNTY COURT   No.

BETWEEN

                                                Plaintiff

and

                                              Defendant

PARTICULARS OF CLAIM

1. The Plaintiff's claim is against the Defendant for an injunction restraining him from committing acts of trespass and nuisance against the Plaintiff

2. The Plaintiff and the Defendant went out together from *[date]* to *[date]*. Once or twice a month the Defendant stayed overnight with the Plaintiff at *[address]* rented in the Plaintiff's sole name from the local authority. On *[date]* the Plaintiff told the Respondent that she regarded the relationship as over.

3. The Defendant has persistently followed and pestered the Plaintiff ever since.

4. On the 2nd April *[year]* the Defendant followed the Plaintiff from home to work in the morning, from work to lunch and back again at lunch time, from work to home in the evening and then from home to her friend's house in the evening. This behaviour was repeated on the 3rd, 5th, 6th, 9th, 10th, 11th and 13th April.

5. On the 5th April, the Defendant approached the Plaintiff as she got into her car and when she refused to speak to him, he kicked the car door causing a dent in the bodywork.

6. On the 9th April, the Plaintiff saw the Defendant doing something to her car and when she examined it later saw that the word "Bitch" was scratched on the bonnet.

7. On numerous occasions, the Defendant has telephoned the Plaintiff at work and at home and on the 10th April he telephoned constantly from 3.00 a.m. until 4.15 a.m. causing her distress and lack of sleep.

8. From about 11.45 p.m. on the 11th April the fire brigade, then the police, then an ambulance, then the emergency gas board people, then a taxi arrived at the Plaintiff's home saying they had received calls to attend. The Plaintiff believes these calls were

made by the Defendant. These hoax calls caused the Plaintiff distress and embarrassment.

9. On the 12th April, the Defendant telephoned the Plaintiff's employer at work, her mother and father at their places of work and also telephoned the Plaintiff at work constantly from 2.00 p.m to 3.00 p.m.

AND the Plaintiff claims:

    (a) an injunction restraining the Defendant from committing acts of nuisance or trespass against the Plaintiff
    (b) costs

Dated the   day of

....

Solicitors for the Plaintiff of

B2. Application for Injunction

> See Form N16A, Appendix, p. 215.

C. Protection from Harassment Act 1997

THE LAW

4-39   Molestation has been said to include such a degree of harassment as would warrant the intervention of the court[20] and so it is likely that a cohabitant or former cohabitant will be able to obtain an order restraining a person from pursuing any conduct which amounts to harassment under Part IV of the Family Law Act. However, an alternative course of action would be under the Protection from Harassment Act. Section 1 says that a person must not pursue a course of conduct which amounts to harassment of another and which he knows or ought to know amounts to harassment of another. He ought to know if a reasonable person in possession of the same information would think the course of conduct amounted to harassment of the other.

4-40   If there is an actual or apprehended breach of section 1, the person who is or may be the victim of the course of conduct can bring a claim in civil proceedings. Damages may be awarded for any anxiety caused by and any financial loss resulting from the harassment.[21]

If the High Court or county court grants an injunction restraining the defendant from pursuing any conduct which amounts to harassment and the plaintiff considers the defendant has done anything which he is prohibited from doing by the injunction, the plaintiff may apply to a High Court judge in the case of a High Court injunction and to a judge or district judge in the case of a county court injunction, for the issue of a warrant for the arrest of the defendant.[22] Furthermore, if, without reasonable excuse, the defendant does anything which he is prohibited from doing by the injunction, he is guilty of an offence[23] punishable on conviction on indictment, to imprisonment for a term not exceeding five years or a fine or both or on summary conviction, to imprisonment for a term, not exceeding six months or a fine not exceeding the statutory maximum or both.[24] and so police officers have the power to arrest without warrant anyone they reasonably suspect of having committed the offence. Where a person is convicted of an offence, his or her conduct is not punishable as a contempt of court and a person cannot be convicted of an offence in respect of any conduct which has been punished as a contempt of court.[25]

---

[20] *Horner v. Horner* [1982] Fam. 90.
[21] s. 3(1) and (2).
[22] s. 3(3). Not yet in force.
[23] s. 3(6). Not yet in force.
[24] s. 3(9). Not yet in force.
[25] s. 3(7), (8). Not yet in force.

The Procedure

The normal rules applicable to fixed date actions apply. In addition, there can be an application for a free-standing injunction on form 16A. **4–41**

The Precedents

The precedents for a civil claim are as set out under section B above. **4–42**

PART V—NON-CONTENTIOUS DOCUMENTS

A. Deed of Separation

THIS DEED OF SEPARATION is made the   day of
BETWEEN *[name]* of *[address]* (Ms.   ) (1) and
          [name] of *[address]* (Mr.   ) (2)

WHEREAS:

(1) Ms.   and Mr.   started living together on the   day of   and have child(ren) namely *[names and dates of birth]*

(2) Differences have arisen between Ms.   and Mr.   as a result of which they have agreed to live separate and apart (and have lived separate and apart) from *[date]*

(3) Ms.   and Mr.   have each taken separate and independent legal advice on the matters referred to in this deed and intend to be legally bound by it.

(4) Mr.   has been paying Ms.   maintenance at the rate of £   per month since *[date]*

(5) The furniture and all other contents of *[address]* have already been divided by agreement between the parties

NOW THIS DEED WITNESSES and it is agreed and declared by and between Ms.   and Mr.   as follows:

1. Mr.   and Ms.   will (continue to) live separate and apart from each other.

2. Neither party will annoy or interfere with the other or his or her relatives, friends, colleagues or business contacts.

3. The home *[address]* shall be sold as soon as reasonably practicable at the best price reasonably obtainable and the solicitors for Mr

shall have conduct of the sale. The net proceeds of sale after redemption of the mortgage in favour of the *[name]* Building Society and payment of the solicitors and estate agents' fees shall be divided (equally between Ms and Mr *or as appropriate*)

4. Mr   shall pay Ms   a lump sum of £   on or before the   day of   and in default shall pay interest at 3% above the   Bank base rate until such time as the said lump sum shall be paid.

5. Ms   shall retain the endowment policies that are presently in her name and Mr   shall retain the endowment policies that are presently in his name.

6. Mr   will pay to Ms   maintenance at the rate of £   per month payable in advance on the 1st day of each month during their joint lives or until Ms
marries or cohabits with another man for a period in excess of six months or until the parties hereto resume cohabitation or until they agree in writing to terminate or vary the said obligation to pay maintenance whichever shall be the earlier.

7. This deed can only be varied by a written agreement executed as a deed by both parties.

SIGNED AS A DEED
by the said
in the presence of

B. Transfer from Joint Names into Sole Name

H.M. LAND REGISTRY
LAND REGISTRATION ACTS 1925 to 1986

County and District or London Borough
Title number
Property
Date

1. In this transfer
1.1 "the Transferor" means *name* of *address*
1.2 "the Transferee" means *name* of *address*
1.3 "the Property" means the land comprised in the above title
[1.4 "the Mortgagee" means *name* of *address*]
[1.5 "the Mortgage" means the Charge dated *date* and registered on *date* of which the Mortgagee is the registered proprietor]

2. Pursuant to an agreement/ order of the   court dated the   day of   the Transferor and the Transferee transfer the Property with full/limited title guarantee to the Transferee [subject to the Mortgage]

[3. The Transferor covenants with the Transferee from the date hereof to pay all moneys due under the Mortgage (whether capital interest or otherwise) and to perform the obligations in the Mortgage on the part of the Transferor and the Transferee and to indemnify the Transferor and his/her estate and effects against all claims and demands arising out of any failure to do so]

4. So as to give the Transferor a full and sufficient indemnity only the Transferee covenants with the Transferor that the Transferee will at all times from the date of this transfer comply with the covenants (referred to in the entries in the charges register or contained in the conveyance/transfer dated   day of   and made between   and   ) so far as they relate to the property and are enforceable and will indemnify the Transferor and his/her estate and effects against all claims and demands arising out of any failure to do so

5. It is certified that this instrument falls within category H in the Schedule to the Stamp Duty (Exempt Instruments) Regulations 1987

SIGNED as a DEED by
in the presence of

C. Assignment of Tenancy with Landlord's Consent

THIS ASSIGNMENT is made the   day of

BETWEEN   *name* of *address* Tenant (1)
           name of *address* Assignee (2) and
           name of *address* Landlord (3)

NOW THIS DEED WITNESSES as follows:

1. Definitions

1.1 "the Premises" means *[describe premises]*

1.2 "the Tenancy Agreement" means a tenancy agreement dated the   day of   and made between the landlord and the tenant

1.3 "the Tenancy" means the weekly/monthly periodic tenancy granted from the   day of   under the Tenancy Agreement

1.4 "the Rent" means the current rent of £   payable under the Tenancy Agreement

2. Recitals

2.1. By the Tenancy Agreement the Premises were let to the Tenant under the Tenancy

2.2 The Tenancy is subject to the terms and conditions in the Tenancy Agreement (except the following terms which have been varied by an agreement dated the   day of

2.3 The Tenant has agreed to assign the Tenancy to the Assignee

2.4 The Landlord has agreed to consent to the said assignment (on the terms set out below)

3. Consent

The Landlord consents to the Assignment

4. Assignment

The Tenant assigns the Tenancy to the Assignee

5. Rent

The Assignee agrees with the Tenant to pay the Rent at the times and in the manner specified in the Tenancy Agreement and to perform and observe all the terms and conditions of the Tenancy Agreement and to indemnify the Tenant against all actions and claims whatsoever on account of any omission to pay the rent or any breach of the terms of the Tenancy Agreement

IN WITNESS etc.

D Change of Name

THIS DEED OF NAME CHANGE made the   day of
by me the undersigned *[Christian names or forenames and assumed name]* of *address*
single/married/widowed/divorced

WITNESSES as follows:

1. I absolutely renounce and abandon the use of my former surname of *original surname* and assume (as from the date of this deed) the surname of *assumed surname*

2. I shall at all times from now on in all records deeds and instruments in writing and in all actions and proceedings and in all dealings and transactions and on all occasions use and sign the name of *assumed surname* as my surname instead of my former name of *original surname* which is renounced

3. I authorise and request all persons to designate and address me by the assumed surname of *assumed surname*

SIGNED AS A DEED
by the above named *assumed name*   formerly known as
original name in the presence of

For use where person has long been known by assumed name

I *Name* of *address* do solemnly and sincerely declare as follows:

1. I am the person named as   in the birth certificate now produced and shown to me marked AB1 ("the Birth Certificate")

2. Since   I have been known by the name of

3. It is my intention from now on in all records deeds and instruments and in all actions and proceedings and in all dealings and transactions and on all occasions to use the name of   and I do renounce for the future the name of   appearing in the Birth Certificate

4. I have authorised all persons to designate and address me by the assumed surname of

AND I make this solemn declaration conscientiously believing the same to be true and by virtue of the Statutory Declarations Act 1835

Declared at
this day of

Before me

Deed of name change for minor

I *name* of *address* mother/father of *name and date of birth of child* do solemnly and sincerely declare as follows:

1. On behalf of *name of child* I absolutely renounce and abandon the use of the former surname of *original surname* and assume (as from the date of this deed) the surname of *assumed surname*

2. On behalf of *name of child* I shall at all times from now on in all records deeds and instruments in writing and in all actions and proceedings and in all dealings and transactions and on all occasions use and sign the name of *assumed name* instead of the former name *original name* which is renounced

3. On behalf of *name of child* I authorise and request all persons to designate and address *name of child* by the assumed surname of *assumed surname*

SIGNED AS A DEED etc.

E. Appointment of testamentary guardian

I *[name of mother, or father with parental responsibility]* of *[address]* in accordance with section 5 Children Act 1989 appoint *[name(s) and address(es) of guardian(s)]* to be the guardian(s) of my child *[name of child]* (and all my children born hereafter) during his/her/their minority.

If (both of) the said guardian(s) shall refuse or for any reason whatsoever cease to act as such guardian(s) then I appoint *[name and address of alternative guardian]* to be such guardian in his/her/their place.

Dated this   day of

....
[Signature]

F. Application under the Criminal Injuries Compensation Scheme

An application form, a guide to the Criminal Injuries Compensation Scheme and a copy of the scheme itself are available from the Criminal Injuries Compensation Authority

> Tay House,
> 300 Bath Street,
> Glasgow G2 4JR

Telephone 0141 331 2726
Fax   0141 331 2287

Appendices

Appendix 1

Forms

Table of Forms

1.	Form C1	Application for an order	158
2.	Form C2	Application [for leave to commence proceedings] [for an order or directions in existing family proceedings] [to be joined as, or cease to be, a party in existing family proceedings]	163
3.	Form C6	Notice of Proceedings [Hearing] [Directions Appointment] (to parties)	165
4.	Form C6A	Notice of Proceedings [Hearing] [Directions Appointment] (to non-parties)	167
5.	Form C7	Acknowledgement	169
6.	Form C9	Statement of Service	171
7.	Form C10	Supplement for an application for financial provision for a child or variation of financial provision for a child.	172
8.	Form C10A	Statement of Means	175
9.	Form C11	Supplement for an application for an Emergency Protection Order	179
10.	Form C23	Emergency Protection Order	181
11.	Form C33	Interim Care Order	183
12.	Form C43	[Residence][Contact][Specific Issue][Prohibited Steps] Order	184
13.	Form C44	Order [Leave to change the surname by which a child is known] [Leave to remove a child from the United Kingdom]	185
14.	Form C45	Order [Parental Responsibility Order] [Termination of a Parental Responsibility Order]	186
15.	Form C46	Order [Appointment of a guardian] [Termination of the appointment of a guardian]	187
16.	Form FL401	Application for [a non-molestation order][an occupation order]	188
17.	Form FL403	Application to vary, extend or discharge an order in existing proceedings	197
18.	Form FL404	Order/Direction	199
19.	Form FL406	Power of arrest	207
20.	Form FL407	Application for a Warrant of Arrest	208
21.	Form FL408	Warrant of Arrest	209
22.	Form FL415	Statement of Service	210
23.	Form FL416	Notice to Mortgagees and Landlords	211
24.	Form FL417	Transfer of Proceedings to [the High Court][a county court] [a family proceedings court]	212
25.	Form N16	Injunction Order	213
26.	Form N16A	Application for Injunction	215
27.	Form C(PRA)(M)	Parental Responsibility Agreement	216

Application for an order

Children Act 1989

Form C1

The court

To be completed by the court

Date issued

Case number

The full name(s) of the child(ren)

Child(ren)'s number(s)

1 About you (the applicant)

State
- your title, full name, address, telephone number, date of birth and relationship to each child above
- your solicitor's name, address, reference, telephone, FAX and DX numbers.

2 The child(ren) and the order(s) you are applying for

For each child state
- the full name, date of birth and sex
- the type of order(s) you are applying for (for example, residence order, contact order, supervision order).

3 Other cases which concern the child(ren)

If there have ever been, or there are pending, any court cases which concern
- *a child whose name you have put in paragraph 2*
- *a full, half or step brother or sister of a child whose name you have put in paragraph 2*
- *a person in this case who is or has been, involved in caring for a child whose name you have put in paragraph 2*

attach a copy of the relevant order and give
- *the name of the court*
- *the name and **panel** address (if known) of the guardian ad litem, if appointed*
- *the name and contact address (if known) of the court welfare officer, if appointed*
- *the name and contact address (if known) of the solicitor appointed for the child(ren).*

4 The respondent(s)

Appendix 3 Family Proceedings Rules 1991; Schedule 2 Family Proceedings Courts (Children Act 1989) Rules 1991

For each respondent state
- *the title, full name and address*
- *the date of birth (if known) or the age*
- *the relationship to each child.*

5 Others to whom notice is to be given

Appendix 3 Family Proceedings Rules 1991; Schedule 2 Family Proceedings Courts (Children Act 1989) Rules 1991

For each person state
- the title, full name and address
- the date of birth (if known) or age
- the relationship to each child

6 The care of the child(ren)

For each child in paragraph 2 state
- the child's current address and how long the child has lived there
- whether it is the child's usual address and who cares for the child there
- the child's relationship to the other children (if any).

7 Social Services

For each child in paragraph 2 state
- whether the child is known to the Social Services.
  If so, give the name of the social worker and the address of the Social Services department.
- whether the child is, or has been, on the Child Protection Register. If so, give the date of registration.

8 The education and health of the child(ren)

For each child state
- *the name of the school, college or place of training which the child attends*
- *whether the child is in good health. Give details of any serious disabilities or ill health.*
- *whether the child has any special needs.*

9 The parents of the child(ren)

For each child state
- *the full name of the child's mother and father*
- *whether the parents are, or have been, married to each other*
- *whether the parents live together. If so, where.*
- *whether, to your knowledge, either of the parents have been involved in a court case concerning a child. If so, give the date and the name of the court.*

10 The family of the child(ren) (other children)

For any other child not already mentioned in the family (for example, a brother or a half sister) state
- *the full name and address*
- *the date of birth (if known) or age*
- *the relationship of the child to you.*

C1

11 Other adults

State
- *the full name of any other adults (for example, lodgers) who live at the same address as any child named in paragraph 2*
- *whether they live there all the time*
- *whether, to your knowledge, the adult has been involved in a court case concerning a child. If so, give the date and the name of the court.*

12 Your reason(s) for applying and any plans for the child(ren)

State briefly your reasons for applying and what you want the court to order.
- *Do not give a full statement if you are applying for an order under Section 8 of Children Act 1989. You may be asked to provide a full statement later.*
- *Do not complete this section if this form is accompanied by a prescribed supplement.*

13 At the court

State
- *whether you will need an interpreter at court (parties are responsible for providing their own). If so, specify the language.*
- *whether disabled facilities will be needed at court.*

Signed   Date
(Applicant)

Application

- **for leave to commence proceedings**
  Family Proceedings Rules 1991 Rule 4.3
  Family Proceedings Courts (Children Act 1989) Rules 1991 Rule 3

- **for an order or directions in existing family proceedings**
  Children Act 1989

- **to be joined as, or cease to be, a party in existing family proceedings**
  Family Proceedings Rules 1991 Rule 4.7(2)
  Family Proceedings Courts (Children Act 1989) Rules 1991 Rule 7(2)

Form C2

The court	To be completed by the court
	Date issued
	Case number
The full name(s) of the child(ren)	Child(ren)'s number(s)

1 About you (the person making this application)

State
- *your title, full name, address, telephone number, date of birth and relationship to each child above*
- *your solicitor's name, address, reference, telephone, FAX and DX numbers*
- *if you are already a party to the case, give your description (for example, applicant, respondent or other).*

2 The order(s) or direction(s) you are applying for

State for each child
- *the full name, date of birth and sex*
- *the type of order(s) you are applying for (for example, residence order, contact order, supervision order).*

3 Persons to be served with this application

For each respondent to this application state the title, full name and address.

4 Your reason(s) for applying and any plans for the child(ren)

State briefly your reasons for applying.
Do not give a full statement if you are applying for an order under Section 8 Children Act 1989. You may be asked to provide a full statement later.

Signed
(Applicant)

Date

APPENDIX 1   165

In

Telephone Number

FAX Number

Case Number

Notice of Proceedings
[Hearing] [Directions Appointment]

                                                    has applied to the court for an order.
The application concerns the following child(ren)   Child(ren)'s number(s)

About the [Hearing] [Directions Appointment]
You should attend when the Court hears the application at

on

at   [am] [pm]

The hearing is estimated to last

What to do next
There is a copy of the application with this Notice. You have been named as a party in the application. Read the application now, and the notes overleaf.

When you go to court please take this Notice with you and show it to a court official.

C6 (Notice to parties)

About this Notice

Note 1 At the hearing or directions appointment — you will be able to tell the Court about any special needs or circumstances of the child(ren).

Note 2 If Form C7 (Acknowledgement) is enclosed — you must fill it in and return it to the court as soon as possible, and serve a copy on the other parties.

Note 3 For legal advice — go to a solicitor or an advice agency.

Some solicitors specialise in court proceedings which involve children. You can obtain the address of a solicitor or an advice agency from the Yellow Pages or the Solicitors' Regional Directory.
You will find these books at
- a Citizens Advice Bureau
- a Law Centre
- a local library.

A solicitor or an advice agency will be able to tell you whether you may be eligible for legal aid.

Note 4 If you want to apply for an order — in respect of any of the children named on the Notice, fill in Form C2. In all correspondence quote the case number and the child(ren)'s number(s).

You can obtain the form from a court office. A booklet is available which will tell you more about the orders you can apply for and help you to make your application. The application must be made to the court sending you this notice.

C6 (Notice to parties)

In

Telephone Number

FAX Number

Case Number

Notice of Proceedings
[Hearing] [Directions Appointment]

has applied to the court for

a

order.

The application concerns the following child(ren)   Child(ren)'s number(s)

About the [Hearing] [Directions Appointment]

The Court will hear the application at

on

at   [am] [pm]

The hearing is estimated to last

What to do next

You have been named in the application. Please read the notes overleaf.

If you go to court please take this Notice with you and show it to a court official.

C6A (Notice to non-parties)

About this Notice

Note 1   **You do not have the right to take part in the proceedings, at present.**
If you want to take part (become a party to the proceedings) you must apply to the court on Form C2. In all correspondence quote the case number and the child(ren)'s number(s).

You can obtain Form C2 from a court office. A booklet is available which will tell you more about the orders you can apply for and help you to make your application. The application must be made to the court sending you this notice.

Note 2   For legal advice go to a solicitor or an advice agency.
Some solicitors specialise in court proceedings which involve children. You can obtain the address of a solicitor or an advice agency from the Yellow Pages or the Solicitors' Regional Directory.
You will find these books at
- a Citizens Advice Bureau
- a Law Centre
- a local library

A solicitor or an advice agency will be able to tell you whether you may be eligible for legal aid.

C6A (Notice to non-parties)

APPENDIX 1   169

Acknowledgement   Form C7

The court

                              Case number

The full name(s) of the child(ren)   Child(ren)'s number(s)

Date of [Hearing] [Directions Appointment]

What you (the person receiving this form) should do

- Answer the questions overleaf.

- If you need more space for an answer use a separate sheet of paper. Please put your full name, case number and the child(ren)'s number(s) at the top.

- If the applicant has asked the court to order you to make a payment for a child you must also fill in a Statement of Means (Form C10A). You can obtain this form from a court office if one has not been enclosed with the papers served on you.

- When you have answered the questions make copies of both sides of this form. You will need a copy for the applicant, and each party named in Part 4 of Form C1.

- Post, or hand, a copy to the applicant and to each party. Then post, or take, this form, and the Statement of Means if you filled one in, to the court at the address below.
  You must do this **within 14 days** of the date when you were given the Notice of Proceedings, or of the postmark on the envelope if the Notice of Proceedings was posted to you.

To be completed by the court

[The Chief Clerk] [Clerk to the Justices]   The court office is open

                                                   from   am to   pm

                                                   on Mondays to Fridays

C7

Appendix 1

1 About you

Full name

Date of birth

Address

Please give a daytime telephone number if you can.

Telephone Number

2 About your solicitor

If you do not have a solicitor put None. (But see note 3 on the Notice of Proceedings which was served on you).

Name

Address

Telephone Number

FAX Number

DX Number

3 Address to which letters and other papers should be sent.

4 The application was received on :

5 Do you oppose the application?

6 Do you intend to apply to the court for an order?

7 Will you use an interpreter at court?

If Yes state the language into which the interpreter will translate.
Note: If you require an interpreter you must bring your own.

Signed
(Respondent)

Date

C7

Statement of Service

Form C9

Family Proceedings Rules 1991 Rule 4.8

Family Proceedings Courts (Children Act 1989) Rules 1991 Rule 8

The court

Case number

The full name(s) of the child(ren)

Child(ren)'s number(s)

You must	- give details of service of the application on each of the other parties
- give details of service on persons to whom notice has to be given
- file this form with the court on or before the first Directions Appointment or Hearing of the Proceedings
You should	- if the person's solicitor was served, give his or her name and address
- if the guardian ad litem was served on behalf of the child, give his or her name and panel address.
You must indicate or	- the manner, date, time and place of service,
- where service was effected by post, the date, time and place of posting.

Name and address of person served	How, when and where served	Prescribed forms served

I have served the [application] [Notice of Proceedings] as stated above.
I am the [applicant] [solicitor for the applicant] [other (state)]

Signed   Date

C9

Supplement for an application for financial provision for a child or variation of financial provision for a child

Paragraph 4 Schedule 1 Children Act 1989

Form C10

The court	To be completed by the court
	Date issued
	Case number
The full name(s) of the child(ren)	Child(ren)'s number(s)

1 About the application

State whether you are seeking
- an order for a lump sum; a transfer of property; a settlement of property; periodical payments; secured periodical payments

or
- a variation of an order for periodical payments; secured periodical payments; payment of a lump sum by instalments.

Note: Applications concerning transfer of property, settlement of property or secured periodical payments can only be heard in the High Court or a county court.

2 Previous court orders and written agreements

If a written agreement or court order has been made a copy should be attached to this application.

If not available state
- the date
- the terms
- the parties
- the court.

3 The Child Support Agency

Assessment for maintenance
State whether the Agency has made an assessment for the maintenance of the child(ren): ☐ Yes ☐ No
If Yes, state whether you are applying for additional child maintenance
- because the Child Support Agency will no longer deal with your claim.
   You should explain why the Agency will not deal with the claim.
or • on top of payments made through the Child Support Agency.
   You should explain why you need additional maintenance and confirm that the Child Support
   Agency's assessment is the maximum amount obtainable.

Written agreement for maintenance
State whether there is a written maintenance agreement: ☐ Yes ☐ No
If No, state whether you are applying for payment:

☐ for [a] stepchild[ren]

☐ in addition to child support maintenance already paid under a Child Support Agency assessment

   ☐ to meet expenses arising from the disability of [a] child[ren]

   ☐ to meet expenses incurred by [a] child[ren] in being educated or training for work

   ☐ when either the child[ren] OR the person with care of the child[ren] OR
      the absent parent of the child[ren] is not habitually resident in the United Kingdom

   ☐ for any other reason *(specify)*:

4 About the order

State the terms of the order you ask the Court to make and in particular
- *the amount you would like the court to order*
- *whether you would like that amount paid weekly or monthly (if you are not applying for a lump sum)*
- *why you require the payments, or would like the court to vary an existing order.*

5 The collection of payment

If payments are not to be collected and paid to you by the Child Support Agency, give full details of how you would like payments collected. Possible ways are:

☐ **Directly to a bank, building society or post office account**
Give the full name and address, sorting code and the number of the account into which payment is to be made.

☐ **By an attachment of earnings order**
This is a court order which is sent to the employer of the person who is to pay.

☐ **If you would like the court to direct that money is paid in some other way**
please say what method you would like.
And if you do not mind how the money is paid, please say so. The Court will decide how it should be paid.

Signed   Date
(Applicant)

You should now complete a Statement of Means, Form C10A

C10

APPENDIX 1   175

Statement of Means	Form C10A
Schedule 1 Children Act 1989	

The court	To be completed by the court
	Date issued
	Case number
The full name(s) of the child(ren)	Child(ren)'s number(s)

Warning   The Court will require to see written evidence of unemployment or sickness; or wage or salary slips, bank statements, and other papers giving details of your means. This evidence should be attached to this form or brought with you when you attend the hearing.

1   About you

State
- *your title, full name, address, telephone number and date of birth*
- *whether you are married, single or other*
- *whether you are the applicant or the respondent.*

2   Your dependants

State for each dependant
- *the dependant's title, full name and age*
- *whether the dependant is a spouse, partner, child or other*
- *whether the dependant is wholly or partially financially dependent on you*
- *whether the dependant lives with you.*

3   Your employment

State whether you are employed, self-employed, unemployed or other.
If you are employed, state
- *your employment*
- *your employer's name, address and daytime telephone number.*

C10A

4 Your buildings and land

List all buildings and land you own, whether in your name alone or jointly, stating for each
- *the address*
- *the name(s) of the owner(s)*
- *the current value.*

5 Your financial assets

List each bank, building society and post office account, stating for each
- *the name and address where the account is held*
- *the account number*
- *the current balance.*

List all investments and securities (for example, shares, insurance policies) stating for each one the name and quantity and current value.

List all pension schemes, stating for each one the scheme name and the company.

6 Other possessions of value

List all possessions of value (for example, jewellery, antiques, collectable items), stating for each:
- *what they are*
- *the current value.*

7 Your income

		State whether Weekly(W) or Monthly(M)
If employed, state your usual take home pay	£	
If self employed, state	• your drawings	£
	• your gross turnover	£
	• your profit after expenses	£
	• whether you expect your turnover to increase, decrease or remain the same:	
	• the date of the accounts showing the above gross turnover and profit after expenses	Year ending 19
In all cases, state any of the following which you receive	• Income support	£
	• Child benefits	£
	• Child Support Agency	£
	• Other state benefits (specify source)	£
		£
		£
	• Pension(s) (specify source)	£
		£
		£
	• Contributions from others in the home (total)	£
	• Other income (specify source and amount)	£
		£
		£
		£
	Total income:	£ _____

8 Court Orders

Enclose a copy of any order

Court	Case Number	Amount outstanding (£)	Amount of payment (£)	Weekly(W) or Monthly(M))

C10A

178   APPENDIX 1

9 Your expenses

	Amount of payments	Weekly (W) or Monthly (M)	Total debt	Amount of arrears
Mortgage				
1st	___	___	___	___
2nd	___	___	___	___
Rent	___	___		___
Council tax	___	___		___
Gas	___	___		___
Electricity	___	___		___
Telephone	___	___		___
Water charges	___	___		___
Credit Card	___	___	___	
Loans	___	___	___	___
Storecards	___	___	___	
HP Payments	___	___	___	___
TV rental and licence	___	___		___
Mail Order	___	___	___	___
Food	___	___		
Clothing	___	___		
Public transport	___	___		
Car expenses	___	___		
School meals	___	___		
Child minding	___	___		
Maintenance	___	___		___
Child Support Agency	___	___		___
Other payments (give details)	___	___	___	___
	___	___	___	___
	___	___	___	___
Total Payments	___	___	___	___

Signed: Date:

[Applicant] [Respondent]

C10A

Supplement for an application for an Emergency Protection Order

Form C11

Section 44 Children Act 1989

The court	To be completed by the court Date issued
The full name(s) of the child(ren)	Case number Child(ren)'s number(s)

1 Description of the child(ren)

If a child's identity is not known, state details which will identify the child.
You may enclose a recent photograph of the child, which should be dated.

2 The grounds for the application

The grounds are

ANY APPLICANT

A ☐ that there is reasonable cause to believe that [this] [these] child[ren] [is] [are] likely to suffer significant harm if

☐ the child[ren] [is] [are] not removed to accommodation provided by or on behalf of this applicant

or ☐ the child[ren] [does] [do] not remain in the place where [the child] [they] [is] [are] currently being accommodated.

LOCAL AUTHORITY APPLICANTS

B ☐ that enquiries are being made about the welfare of the child[ren] under Section 47(1)(b) of Children Act 1989 **and** those enquiries are being frustrated by access to the child[ren] being unreasonably refused to someone who is authorised to seek access **and** there is reasonable cause to believe that access to the child[ren] is required as a matter of urgency.

AUTHORISED PERSON APPLICANTS

C ☐ that there is reasonable cause to suspect that the child[ren] [is] [are] suffering, or [is] [are] likely to suffer, significant harm **and** enquiries are being made with respect to the welfare of the child[ren] **and** those enquiries are being frustrated by access to the child[ren] being unreasonably refused to someone who is authorised to seek access **and** there is reasonable cause to believe that access to the child[ren] is required as a matter of urgency.

3 **The additional order(s) applied for**

☐ *information on the whereabouts of the child[ren] (Section 48(1) Children Act 1989).*

☐ *authorisation for entry of premises (Section 48(3) Children Act 1989).*

☐ *authorisation to search for another child on the premises (Section 48(4) Children Act 1989).*

4 **The direction(s) sought**

☐ *contact (Section 44(6)(a) Children Act 1989).*

☐ *a medical or psychiatric examination or other assessment of the child[ren] (Section 44(6)(b) Children Act 1989).*

☐ *to be accompanied by a registered medical practitioner, registered nurse or registered health visitor (Section 45(12) Children Act 1989).*

☐ *an exclusion requirement (Section 44A(1) Children Act 1989).*

5 **The reason(s) for the application**

If you are relying on a report or other documentary evidence, state the date(s) and author(s) and enclose a copy.

Signed   Date
(Applicant)

APPENDIX 1   181

 In the

Case Number:

Child(ren)'s Number(s):

Order   Emergency Protection Order
Section 44 Children Act 1989

The full name(s) of the child(ren)	Boy or Girl	Date(s) of birth

[described as

Warning   It is an offence intentionally to obstruct any person exercising the power under Section 44(4)(b) Children Act 1989 to remove, or prevent the removal, of a child (Section 44(15) Children Act 1989).

The Court grants   an Emergency Protection Order to the applicant who is

The Order gives the applicant parental responsibility for the child[ren].

The Court authorises   [the applicant to remove the child[ren] to accommodation provided by or on behalf of the applicant]
[the applicant to prevent the child[ren] being removed from

[This order directs that   any person who can produce the child[ren] to the applicant must do so.]

The Court directs that   [[a named person] to be excluded from [a named address] [forthwith] [from [date]] so that the child may continue to live there, consent to the exclusion requirement having been given by [a named person]]

[a power of arrest be attached to the exclusion requirement for a period of]

This order ends on   at   [am] [pm]

Ordered by   [Mr] [Mrs] Justice
[His] [Her] Honour Judge
District Judge [of Family Division]
Justice[s] of the Peace

on   at   [am] [pm]

C23

Notes about the Emergency Protection Order

About this order   This is an Emergency Protection Order.
This order states what has been authorised in respect of the child[ren] and when the order will end.
The court can extend this order for up to 7 days but it can only do this once.

Warning   **If you are shown this order, you must comply with it. If you do not, you may commit an offence. Read the order now.**

What you may do   You may apply to the court
        to **change the directions**
or   to **end the order.**

You may apply at any time, but the court will only hear an application to end an order **when 72 hours** have passed since the order was made.
If you would like to ask the court to change the directions, or end the order, you must fill in a form. You can obtain the form from a court office.

If the court has directed that the child[ren] should have a medical, psychiatric or another kind of examination, you may ask the court to allow a doctor of your choice to be at the examination.

What you should do   Go to a solicitor as soon as you can.

Some solicitors specialise in court proceedings which involve children. You can obtain the address of a solicitor or advice agency from the Yellow Pages or the Solicitor's Regional Directory.

You will find these books at
- a Citizens Advice Bureau
- a Law Centre
- a local library

A solicitor or an advice agency will be able to tell you whether you may be eligible for legal aid.

APPENDIX 1 183

In the

Case Number:

Child(ren)'s Number(s):

Order   Interim Care Order
        Section 38 Children Act 1989

        The full name(s) of the child(ren)   Date(s) of birth

The Court orders   that the child[ren] be placed in the care of

                                                                local authority

The order expires on

The Court directs   [[a named person] be excluded from [a named address] [forthwith] [from [date]] so that the child may continue to live there, consent to the exclusion requirement having been given by [a named person]].

[a power of arrest be attached to the exclusion requirement for a period of   ]

Warning   While a Care Order is in force no person may cause the child[ren] to be known by a new surname or remove the child[ren] from the United Kingdom without the written consent of every person with parental responsibility for the child[ren] or the leave of the court.

However, the local authority, in whose care a child is, may remove that child from the United Kingdom for a period of less than 1 month.

It may be a criminal offence under the Child Abduction Act 1984 to remove the child[ren] from the United Kingdom without the leave of the Court.

Ordered by   [Mr] [Mrs] Justice
             [His] [Her] Honour Judge
             District Judge [of the Family Division]
             Justice[s] of the Peace
             Clerk of the Court

        on

C33

184 APPENDIX 1

 In the

Case Number:

Child(ren)'s Number(s):

Order	[Residence] [Contact] [Specific Issue] [Prohibited Steps] Order
	Section 8 Children Act 1989

The full name(s) of the child(ren)	Date(s) of birth

The Court orders

Warning	Where a Residence Order is in force no person may cause the child[ren] to be known by a new surname or remove the child[ren] from the United Kingdom without the written consent of every person with parental responsibility for the child[ren] or the leave of the court.
	However, this does not prevent the removal of [a] child[ren], for a period of less than 1 month, by the person in whose favour the Residence Order is made (Sections 13(1) and (2) Children Act 1989).
	It may be a criminal offence under the Child Abduction Act 1984 to remove the child[ren] from the United Kingdom without the leave of the Court.
Notice	Any person with parental responsibility for [a] child[ren] may obtain advice on what can be done to prevent the issue of a passport to the child[ren]. They should write to The United Kingdom Passport Agency, Clive House, Petty France, LONDON SW1H 9HD.
Ordered by	[Mr] [Mrs] Justice
	[His] [Her] Honour Judge
	District Judge [of the Family Division]
	Justice[s] of the Peace
	[Assistant] Recorder
on	

C43

 In the

Case Number:

Child(ren)'s Number(s):

Order [Leave to change the surname by which a child is known
Section [13(1)] [33(7)] Children Act 1989]

[Leave to remove a child from the United Kingdom
Section [13(1)] [33(7)] Children Act 1989]

The full name(s) of the child(ren)   Date(s) of birth

The Court grants leave to

[to change the child[ren]'s surname to

[and] [to remove the child[ren]]   from the United Kingdom

[permanently] [until

Ordered by   [Mr] [Mrs] Justice
[His] [Her] Honour Judge
District Judge [of the Family Division]
Justice[s] of the Peace
[Assistant] Recorder

on

C44

186 APPENDIX 1

 In the

Case Number:

Child(ren)'s Number(s):

Order [Parental Responsibility Order
Section 4(1) Children Act 1989]

[Termination of a Parental Responsibility Order
Section 4(3) Children Act 1989]

The full name(s) of the child(ren)	Date(s) of birth

The Court orders that

shall [no longer] have parental responsibility for the child[ren].

Notice   A parental responsibility order can only end
a) When the child reaches 18 years
b) By order of the court made
- on the application of any person who has parental responsibility
- with leave of the court on application of the child.

Ordered by   [Mr] [Mrs] Justice
[His] [Her] Honour Judge
District Judge [of the Family Division]
Justice[s] of the Peace
[Assistant] Recorder

on

C45

APPENDIX 1   187

In the

Case Number:

Child(ren)'s Number(s):

Order   [Appointment of a guardian
           Section 5(1) Children Act 1989]

           [Termination of the appointment of a guardian
           Section 6(7) Children Act 1989]

           The full name(s) of the child(ren)   Date(s) of birth

[The Court appoints
                    to be the guardian of the child[ren].

This appointment will begin on   ]

[The Court orders that   the appointment of

                          as guardian for the child[ren] be terminated.]

           Ordered by   [Mr] [Mrs] Justice
                         [His] [Her] Honour Judge
                         District Judge [of the Family Division]
                         Justice[s] of the Peace
                         [Assistant] Recorder

                 on

C46

Appendix 1

Application for:
a non-molestation order
an occupation order

Family Law Act 1996 (Part IV)

The Court

To be completed by the court

Date issued

Case number

Please read the accompanying notes as you complete this form.

1 About you (the applicant)

State your title (Mr, Mrs etc), full name, address, telephone number and date of birth (if under 18):

State your solicitor's name, address, reference, telephone, FAX and DX numbers:

2 About the respondent

State the respondent's name, address and date of birth (if known):

3 The Order(s) for which you are applying

This application is for:

☐ a non-molestation order

☐ an occupation order

☐ Tick this box if you wish the court to hear your application without notice being given to the respondent. The reasons relied on for an application being heard without notice must be stated in the statement in support.

FL401 Application for: a non-molestation order / an occupation order

4 Your relationship to the respondent (the person to be served with this application)

Your relationship to the respondent is:
Please tick only one of the following

1 ☐ Married
2 ☐ Were married
3 ☐ Cohabiting
4 ☐ Were cohabiting

5 ☐ Both of you live or have lived in the same household

6 ☐ Relative
State how related:

7 ☐ Agreed to marry.
Give the date the agreement was made. If the agreement has ended, state when.

8 ☐ Both of you are parents of or have parental responsibility for a child

9 ☐ One of you is a parent of a child and the other has parental responsibility for that child

10 ☐ One of you is the natural parent or
grandparent of a child adopted or
freed for adoption, and the other is:
    (i) the adoptive parent
or (ii) a person who has applied for
an adoption order for the child
or (iii) a person with whom the child
has been placed for adoption
or (iv) the child who has been adopted
or freed for adoption.
State whether (i), (ii), (iii) or (iv):

11 ☐ Both of you are parties to the same family
proceedings (see also Section 11 below).

5 Application for a non-molestation order

If you wish to apply for a non-molestation order, state briefly in this section the order you want.

Give full details in support of your application in your supporting evidence

6 Application for an occupation order

If you do not wish to apply for an occupation order, please go to section 9 of this form.

(A) State the address of the dwelling house to which your application relates:

(B) State whether it is occupied by you or the respondent now or in the past, or whether it was intended to be occupied by you or the respondent:

(C) State whether you are entitled to occupy the dwelling-house: ☐ Yes ☐ No

If yes, explain why:

(D) State whether the respondent is entitled to occupy the dwelling-house: ☐ Yes ☐ No

If yes, explain why:

On the basis of your answer to (C) and (D) above, tick one of the boxes 1 to 5 below to show the category into which you fit

1 ☐ a spouse who has matrimonial home rights in the dwelling-house, or a person who is entitled to occupy it by virtue of a beneficial estate or interest or contract or by virtue of any enactment giving him or her the right to remain in occupation.

If you tick box 1, state whether there is a dispute or pending proceedings between you and the respondent about your right to occupy the dwelling-house.

2 ☐ a former spouse with no existing right to occupy, where the respondent spouse is entitled.

3 ☐ a cohabitant or former cohabitant with no existing right to occupy, where the respondent cohabitant or former cohabitant is so entitled.

4 ☐ a spouse or former spouse who is not entitled to occupy, where the respondent spouse or former spouse is also not entitled.

5 ☐ a cohabitant or former cohabitant who is not entitled to occupy, where the respondent cohabitant or former cohabitant is also not entitled.

Matrimonial Home Rights

If you do have matrimonial home rights please:

State whether the title to the land is registered or unregistered (if known):

If registered, state the Land Registry title number (if known):

If you wish to apply for an occupation order, state briefly here the order you want. Give full details in support of your application in your supporting evidence.

7 Application for additional order(s) about the dwelling house

If you want to apply for any of the orders listed in the notes to this section, state what order you would like the court to make:

8 Mortgage and rent

Is the dwelling house subject to a mortgage?

☐ Yes ☐ No

If yes, please provide the name and address of the mortgagee:

Is the dwelling house rented?

☐ Yes ☐ No

If yes, please provide the name and address of the landlord:

9 At the court

Will you need an interpreter at court?

☐ Yes   ☐ No

If 'Yes', specify the language:

If you need an interpreter because you do not speak English, you are responsible for providing your own.

If you need an interpreter or other facilities because of a disability, please contact the court to ask what help is available.

10 Other information

State the name and date of birth of any child living with or staying with, or likely to live with or stay with, you or the respondent:

State the name of any other person living in the same household as you and the respondent, and say why they live there:

11 Other Proceedings and Orders

If there are any other current family proceedings or orders in force involving you and the respondent, state the type of proceedings or orders, the court and the case number. This includes any application for an occupation order or non-molestation order against you by the respondent.

This application is to be served upon the respondent

Signed   Date

Application for a non-molestation order or occupation order
Notes for Guidance

Section 1

If you do not wish your address to be made known to the respondent, leave the space on the form blank and complete Confidential Address Form C8. The court can give you this form.

If you are under 18, someone over 18 must help you make this application. That person, who might be one of your parents, is called a 'next friend'.

If you are under 16 you need permission to make this application. You must apply to the High Court for permission, using this form. If the High Court gives you permission to make this application, it will then either hear the application itself or transfer it to a county court.

Section 3

An urgent order made by the court before notice of the application is served on the respondent is called an ex-parte order. In deciding whether to make an ex-parte order the court will consider all the circumstances of the case, including:

- *any risk of significant harm to the applicant or a relevant child, attributable to conduct of the respondent, if the order is not made immediately*
- *whether it is likely that the applicant will be deterred or prevented from pursuing the application if an order is not made immediately*
- *whether there is reason to believe that the respondent is aware of the proceedings but is deliberately evading service and that the applicant or a relevant child will be seriously prejudiced by the delay involved.*

If the court makes an ex-parte order, it must give the respondent an opportunity to make representations about the order as soon as just and convenient at a full hearing.

'Harm' in relation to a person who has reached the age of 18 means ill-treatment or the impairment of health, and in relation to a child means ill-treatment or the impairment of health and development. 'Ill-treatment' includes forms of ill-treatment which are not physical and, in relation to a child, includes sexual abuse. The court will require evidence of any harm which you allege in support of your application. This evidence should be included in the statement accompanying this application.

Section 4

For you to be able to apply for an order you must be related to the respondent in one of the ways listed in this section of the form. If you are not related in one of these ways you should seek legal advice.

Cohabitants are a man and a woman who, although not married to each other, are living or have lived together as husband and wife. People who have cohabited, but have then married will not fall within this category, but will fall within the category of married people.

Those who live or have lived in the same household do not include people who share the same household because one of them is the other's employee, tenant, lodger or boarder.

You will only be able to apply as a relative of the respondent if you are:

(A) the father, mother, stepfather, stepmother, son, daughter, stepson, stepdaughter, grandmother, grandfather, grandson or granddaughter of the respondent or of the respondent's spouse or former spouse.

(B) the brother, sister, uncle, aunt, niece or nephew (whether of the full blood or of the half blood or by marriage) of the respondent or of the respondent's spouse or former spouse.

This includes, in relation to a person who is living or has lived with another person as husband and wife, any person who would fall within (A) or (B) if the parties were married to each other (for example, your cohabitee's father or brother).

Agreements to marry: You will fall within this category only if you make this application within three years of the termination of the agreement. The court will require the following evidence of the agreement:

   evidence in writing

   or the gift of an engagement ring in contemplation of marriage

   or evidence that a ceremony has been entered into in the presence of one or more other persons assembled for the purpose of witnessing it.

Parents and parental responsibility: You will fall within this category if

   both you and the respondent are either the parents of a child or have parental responsibility for that child

or if one of you is the parent and the other has parental responsibility.

Under the Children Act 1989, parental responsibility is held automatically by a child's mother, and by the child's father if he and the mother were married to each other at the time of the child's birth or have married subsequently. Where this is not the case, parental responsibility can be acquired by the father in accordance with the provisions of the Children Act 1989.

Section 5

A non-molestation order can forbid the respondent to molest you or a relevant child. Molestation can include, for example, violence, threats, pestering and other forms of harassment. The court can forbid particular acts of the respondent, molestation in general, or both.

Section 6

If you wish to apply for an occupation order but you are uncertain about your answer to any of the questions in this part of the application form, you should seek legal advice.

(A) A dwelling-house includes any building or part of a building which is occupied as a dwelling; any caravan, houseboat or structure which is occupied as a dwelling; and any yard, garden, garage or outhouse belonging to it and occupied with it.

Section 6 (continued)

(C) & (D) *The following questions give examples to help you to decide if you or the respondent, or both of you, are entitled to occupy the dwelling-house:*

(a) Are you the sole legal owner of the dwelling-house?

(b) Are you and the respondent joint legal owners of the dwelling-house?

(c) Is the respondent the sole legal owner of the dwelling-house?

(d) Do you rent the dwelling-house as sole tenant?

(e) Do you and the respondent rent the dwelling-house as joint tenants?

(f) Does the respondent rent the dwelling house as sole tenant?

If you answer
- *Yes to (a), (b), (d) or (e) you are likely to be entitled to occupy the dwelling-house*
- *Yes to (c) or (f) you may not be entitled (unless, for example, you are a spouse and have matrimonial home rights - see the notes under 'Matrimonial Home Rights' below)*
- *Yes to (b), (c), (e) or (f), the respondent is likely to be entitled to occupy the dwelling-house.*
- *Yes to (a) or (d) the respondent may not be entitled (unless, for example, he is a spouse and has matrimonial home rights).*

Box 1 *For example, if you are sole owner, joint owner, or if you rent the property. If you are not a spouse, former spouse, cohabitant or former cohabitant of the respondent, you will only be able to apply for an occupation order if you fall within this category.*

If you answer Yes to this question, it will not be possible for a magistrates' court to deal with the application, unless the court decides that it is unnecessary for it to decide this question in order to deal with the application or make an order. If the court decides that it cannot deal with the application, it will transfer the application to a county court.

Box 2 *For example, if the respondent was married to you and is sole owner or rents the property.*

Box 3 *For example, if the respondent is or was cohabiting with you and is sole owner or rents the property.*

Matrimonial Home Rights

Where one spouse is entitled to occupy the dwelling-house by virtue of a beneficial estate or interest or contract or by virtue of any enactment giving him or her the right to remain in occupation, and the other spouse is not so entitled, the spouse who is not entitled has matrimonial home rights. These are a right, if the spouse is in occupation, not to be evicted or excluded from the dwelling house except with the leave of the court and, if the spouse is not in occupation, the right with the leave of the court to enter into and occupy the dwelling-house.

Matrimonial home rights do not exist if the dwelling-house has never been, and was never intended to be, the matrimonial home of the two spouses. If the marriage has come to an end, matrimonial home rights will also have ceased, unless a court order has been made during the marriage for the rights to continue after the end of the marriage.

Occupation Orders *The possible orders are:*

If you have ticked box 1 above, an order under section 33 of the Act may:

- *enforce the applicant's entitlement to remain in occupation as against the respondent*
- *require the respondent to permit the applicant to enter and remain in the dwelling-house or part of it*
- *regulate the occupation of the dwelling-house by either or both parties*
- *if the respondent is also entitled to occupy, the order may prohibit, suspend or restrict the exercise by him, of that right*
- *restrict or terminate any matrimonial home rights of the respondent*
- *require the respondent to leave the dwelling-house or part of it*
- *exclude the respondent from a defined area around the dwelling-house*
- *declare that the applicant is entitled to occupy the dwelling-house or has matrimonial home rights in it*
- *provide that matrimonial home rights of the applicant are not brought to an end by the death of the other spouse or termination of the marriage.*

If you have ticked box 2 or box 3 above, an order under section 35 or 36 of the Act may:

- *give the applicant the right not to be evicted or excluded from the dwelling-house or any part of it by the respondent for a specified period*
- *prohibit the respondent from evicting or excluding the applicant during that period*
- *give the applicant the right to enter and occupy the dwelling house for a specified period*
- *require the respondent to permit the exercise of that right*
- *regulate the occupation of the dwelling-house by either or both of the parties*
- *prohibit, suspend or restrict the exercise by the respondent of his right to occupy*
- *require the respondent to leave the dwelling-house or part of it*
- *exclude the respondent from a defined area around the dwelling-house.*

If you have ticked box 4 or box 5 above, an order under section 37 or 38 of the Act may:

- *require the respondent to permit the applicant to enter and remain in the dwelling-house or part of it*
- *regulate the occupation of the dwelling-house by either or both of the parties*
- *require the respondent to leave the dwelling-house or part of it*
- *exclude the respondent from a defined area around the dwelling-house.*

Section 6 (continued)

You should provide any evidence which you have on the following matters in your evidence in support of this application. If necessary, further statements may be submitted after the application has been issued.

If you have ticked box 1, 4 or 5 above, the court will need any available evidence of the following:

- the housing needs and resources of you, the respondent and any relevant child
- the financial resources of you and the respondent
- the likely effect of any order, or of any decision not to make an order, on the health, safety and well-being of you, the respondent and any relevant child
- the conduct of you and the respondent in relation to each other and otherwise.

If you have ticked box 2 above, the court will need any available evidence of:

- the housing needs and resources of you, the respondent and relevant child
- the financial resources of you and the respondent
- the likely effect of any order, or of any decision not to make an order, on the health, safety and well-being of you, the respondent and any relevant child
- the conduct of you and the respondent in relation to each other and otherwise.
- the length of time that has elapsed since you and the respondent ceased to live together
- the length of time that has elapsed since the marriage was dissolved or annulled
- the existence of any pending proceedings between you and the respondent:
    under section 23A of the Matrimonial Causes Act 1973 (property adjustment orders in connection with divorce proceedings etc.
    or under Schedule 1 para 1(2)(d) or (e) of the Children Act 1989 (orders for financial relief against parents)
    or relating to the legal or beneficial ownership of the dwelling-house.

If you have ticked box 3 above, the court will need any available evidence of:

- the housing needs and resources of you, the respondent and any relevant child
- the financial resources of you and the respondent
- the likely effect of any order, or of any decision not to make an order, on the health, safety and well-being of you, the respondent and any relevant child
- the conduct of you and the respondent in relation to each other and otherwise
- the nature of you and the respondent's relationship

- the length of time which you have lived together as husband and wife
- whether you and the respondent have had any children, or have both had parental responsibility for any children
- the length of time which has elapsed since you and the respondent ceased to live together
- the existence of any pending proceedings between you and the respondent under Schedule 1 para 1(2)(d) or (e) of the Children Act 1989 or relating to the legal or beneficial ownership of the dwelling-house.

Section 7

Under section 40 of the Act the court may make the following additional orders when making an occupation order:

- impose on either party obligations as to the repair and maintenance of the dwelling-house
- impose on either party obligations as to the payment of rent, mortgage or other outgoings affecting it
- order a party occupying the dwelling-house to make periodical payments to the other party in respect of the accommodation, if the other party would (but for the order) be entitled to occupy it
- grant either party possession or use of furniture or other contents
- order either party to take reasonable care of any furniture or other contents
- order either party to take reasonable steps to keep the dwelling-house and any furniture or other contents secure.

Section 8

If the dwelling-house is rented or subject to a mortgage, the landlord or mortgagee must be served with notice of the proceedings in Form FL416. He or she will then be able to make representations to the court regarding the rent or mortgage.

Section 10

A person living in the same household may, for example, be a member of the family or a tenant or employee of you or the respondent.

Application to vary, extend or discharge an order in existing proceedings
Family Law Act 1996 (Part IV)

To be completed by the court

Date issued

The court to which you are applying:
Note: you must make this application to the court which made the original order.

Case number

---

1 About you (the applicant)

State your title, full name, address, telephone number and date of birth (if under 18).

If you do not wish your address to be made known to the respondent, leave this space blank and complete Confidential Address Form C8 (if you have not already done so). The court can give you this form.

State your solicitor's name, address, reference, telephone, FAX and DX numbers.

If you are already a party to the case, give your description (for example, applicant, respondent or other).

2 The order(s) for which you are applying *Please attach a copy of the order if possible.*

I am applying to   vary   ☐
                extend   ☐
                discharge ☐

the order dated:

If you are applying for an order to be varied or extended please give details of the order which you would like the court to make:

FL403 Application to vary, extend or discharge an order in existing proceedings

3 Your reason(s) for applying

State briefly your reasons for applying.

4 Person(s) to be served with this application

For each respondent to this application state
the title, full name and address.

Signed
(Applicant)

Date

In the

Case Number

[Order]   [Direction]   Sheet   of
Family Law Act 1996

Appendix 1

In the

Case Number

[Order] [Direction] Sheet of
Family Law Act 1996

Ordered by [Mr] [Mrs] Justice
[His] [Her] Honour Judge
[Deputy] District Judge [of the Family Division]
Justice[s] of the Peace
[Assistant] Recorder
Clerk of the Court

on

FL404 Order or Direction

Orders under Family Law Act 1996 Part IV

(General heading followed by Notice A or Notice B and numbered options as appropriate)

<u>Notice A - order includes non-molestation order - penal notice mandatory</u>

Important Notice to the Respondent [name]

This order gives you instructions which you must follow. You should read it all carefully. If you do not understand anything in this order you should go to a solicitor, Legal Advice Centre or Citizens Advice Bureau. You have a right to ask the court to change or cancel the order but you must obey it unless the court does change or cancel it.

You must obey the instructions contained in this order. If you do not, you will be guilty of contempt of court, and you may be sent to prison.

<u>Notice B - order does not include non-molestation order - * penal notice discretionary</u>

Important Notice to the Respondent [name]

This order gives you instructions which you must follow. You should read it all carefully. If you do not understand anything in this order you should go to a solicitor, Legal Advice Centre or Citizens Advice Bureau. You have a right to ask the court to change or cancel the order but you must obey it unless the court does change or cancel it.

You must obey the instructions contained in this order. *[If you do not, you will be guilty of contempt of court, and you may be sent to prison.]

Occupation orders under s33 of the Family Law Act 1996

1. The court declares that the applicant [name] is entitled to occupy [*address of home or intended home*] as [*his/her*] home. **OR**

2. The court declares that the applicant [name] has matrimonial home rights in [*address of home or intended home*]. **AND/OR**

3. The court declares that the applicant [name]'s matrimonial home rights shall not end when the respondent [name] dies or their marriage is dissolved and shall continue until........or further order.

It is ordered that:

4. The respondent [name] shall allow the applicant [name] to occupy [*address of home or intended home*] **OR**

5. The respondent [name] shall allow the applicant [name] to occupy part of [*address of home or intended home*] namely: [*specify part*]

6. The respondent [name] shall not obstruct, harass or interfere with the applicant [name]'s peaceful occupation of [*address of home or intended home*]

7. The respondent [name] shall not occupy [*address of home or intended home*] **OR**

8. The respondent [name] shall not occupy [*address of home or intended home*] from [*specify date*] until [*specify date*] **OR**

9. The respondent [name] shall not occupy [*specify part of address of home or intended home*] **AND/OR**

10. The respondent [name] shall not occupy [*address or part of address*] between [*specify dates or times*]

11. The respondent [name] shall leave [*address or part of address*] [forthwith] [within ____ [*hours/days*] of service on [*him/her*] of this order.] **AND/OR**

12. Having left [*address or part of address*], the respondent [name] shall not return to, enter or attempt to enter [or go within [*specify distance*] of] it.

Occupation orders under ss35 & 36 of the Family Law Act 1996

It is ordered that

13. The applicant [name] has the right to occupy [*address of home or intended home*] and the respondent [name] shall allow the applicant [name] to do so. **OR**

14. The respondent [name] shall not evict or exclude the applicant[name] from [*address of home or intended home*] or any part of it namely [*specify part*]. **AND/OR**

15. The respondent [name] shall not occupy [*address of home or intended home*]. **OR**

16. The respondent [name] shall not occupy [*address of home or intended home*] from [*specify date*] until [*specify date*] **OR**

17. The respondent [name] shall not occupy [*specify part of address of home or intended home*] **OR**

18. The respondent [name] shall leave [*address or part of address*] [forthwith] [within ____ [*hours/days*] of service on [*him/her*] of this order.] **AND/OR**

19. Having left [*address or part of address*], the respondent [name] shall not return to, enter or attempt to enter [or go within [*specify distance*] of] it.

Occupation orders under ss37 & 38 Family Law Act 1996

It is ordered that

20. The respondent [name] shall allow the applicant [name] to occupy [*address of home or intended home*] or part of it namely: [*specify*]. **AND/OR**

21. [One or both of the provisions in paragraphs 6 & 10 above may be inserted] **AND/OR**

22. The respondent [name] shall leave [*address or part of address*] [forthwith] [within ____ [*hours/days*] of service on [*him/her*] of this order]. **AND/OR**

23. Having left [*address or part of address*], the respondent [name] may not return to, enter or attempt to enter [or go within [*specify distance*] of] it.

Additional provisions which may be included in occupation orders made under ss33, 35 or 36 of Family Law Act 1996

It is ordered that

24. The [applicant [name]] [respondent [name]] shall maintain and repair [address of home or intended home] **AND/OR**

25. The [applicant [name]] [respondent [name]] shall pay the rent for [address of home or intended home]. **OR**

26. The [applicant [name]] [respondent [name]] shall pay the mortgage payments on [address of home or intended home]. **OR**

27. The [applicant [name]] [respondent [name]] shall pay the following for [address of home or intended home]: [specify outgoings as bullet points].

28. The [party in occupation] shall pay to the [other party] £   each [week, month, etc] for [address of home etc].

29. The [party in occupation] shall keep and use the [furniture] [contents] [specify if necessary] of [address of home or intended home] and the [applicant [name]] [respondent [name]] shall return to the [party in occupation] the [furniture] [contents] [specify if necessary] [no later than [date/time]].

30. The [party in occupation] shall take reasonable care of the [furniture] [contents] [specify if necessary] of [address of home or intended home].

31. The [party in occupation] shall take all reasonable steps to keep secure [address of home or intended home] and the furniture or other contents [specify if necessary].

Duration

Occupation orders under s33 of the Family Law Act 1996

32. This order shall last until [*specify event or date*]. **OR**

33. This order shall last until a further order is made.

Occupation orders under ss35 & 37 of the Family Law Act 1996

34. This order shall last until [*state date which must not be more than 6 months from the date of this order*].

35. The occupation order made on [*state date*] is extended until [*state date which must not be more than 6 months from the date of this extension*].

Occupation orders under ss36 & 38 Family Law Act 1996

36. This order shall last until [*state date which must not be more than 6 months from the date of this order*].

37. The occupation order made on [*state date*] is extended until [*state date which must not be more than 6 months from the date of this extension*] and must end on that date.

Non-molestation orders

It is ordered that

38. The respondent [name] is forbidden to use or threaten violence against the applicant [name] [and must not instruct, encourage or in any way suggest that any other person should do so]. AND/OR

39. The respondent [name] is forbidden to intimidate, harass or pester [or [specify]] the applicant [name] [and must not instruct, encourage or in any way suggest that any other person should do so]. AND/OR

40. The respondent [name] is forbidden to use or threaten violence against the relevant child(ren) [name(s)and date(s) of birth] [and must not instruct, encourage or in any way suggest that any other person should do so]. AND/OR

41. The respondent [name] is forbidden to intimidate, harass or pester [or [specify]][the relevant child(ren) [name(s) and date(s) of birth] [and must not instruct, encourage or in any way suggest that any other person should do so].

In the

Case Number

Power of Arrest
Family Law Act 1996

Applicant
Ref.
Respondent
Ref

The Court orders that a power of arrest applies to the following paragraph(s) of an order made under this Act on the

(here set out those provisions of the order to which this power of arrest is attached and no others)

Power of Arrest The court is satisfied that the respondent has used or threatened violence against the [applicant] [[and] [or] the following child[ren]

]
[and that there is a risk of significant harm to the applicant [[and] [or] the above child[ren]] attributable to the conduct of the respondent if the power of arrest is not attached immediately].
A power of arrest is attached to the order whereby any constable may (under the power given by section 47(6) of the Family Law Act 1996) arrest without warrant the respondent if the constable has any reasonable cause for suspecting that the respondent may be in breach of any provision to which the power of arrest is attached.

This Power of Arrest expires on

Note to the Arresting Officer Where the respondent is arrested under the power given by section 47 of the Family Law Act 1996, that section requires that:

    the respondent must be brought before the court within 24 hours of the time of his arrest
and if the matter is not then disposed of forthwith, the court may remand the respondent.

Nothing in section 47 authorises the detention of the respondent after the expiry of the period of 24 hours beginning at the time of his arrest, unless remanded by the court.
The period of 24 hours shall not include Christmas Day, Good Friday or a Sunday.

Ordered by [Mr] [Mrs] Justice

[His] [Her] Honour Judge

[Deputy]District Judge [of the Family Division]

Justice[s] of the Peace

[Assistant] Recorder

on

FL406 Power of Arrest

APPENDIX 1

In the

Case Number

Application for a Warrant of Arrest

Applicant
Ref.
Respondent
Ref.

(1) Set out the precise parts of the order or undertaking relevant to this application

On the   day of   19   , the Court made an order [*or* the respondent gave an undertaking] as follows:(1)

(2) Insert name of applicant

I, (2)   apply for an order that a warrant should be issued for the arrest of the

(3) Insert name of person against whom the warrant of arrest is sought

respondent(3)

(4) List the ways in which it is alleged that the respondent has disobeyed the order or broken the undertaking. If necessary continue on a separate sheet

The respondent has disobeyed the order [or broken the undertaking] by (4)

Signed   Date

FL407 Application for a warrant of arrest

In the

Case Number

Warrant of Arrest
Family Law Act 1996

	Applicant
	Ref.
	Respondent
	Ref

The Court directs all police constables, [the district judge and bailiffs] [and the Tipstaff of the High Court] to arrest the respondent whose address is [believed to be]:

and to bring the respondent before this court immediately.

The Court heard an application, supported by [sworn written statement] [evidence on oath], that the respondent had disobeyed the order made

on

at the [Magistrates'] [County] [High] Court

by

[Notice of bail] On arrest, the respondent shall be released on bail:

- on entering into a recognizance in the sum of [£   ]
- [and on providing [   ] suret[y] [ies] in the sum of [£   ] and [£   ]]
- [and subject to the following conditions:

]

The Next Hearing is [on   at   [am] [pm]]
[on a day and at a time to be specified]]

Ordered by [Mr] [Mrs] Justice
[His] [Her] Honour Judge
District Judge [of the Family Division]
Justice[s] of the Peace
[Assistant] Recorder

on

FL408 Warrant of Arrest

Statement of Service
Family Law Act 1996

	Case number
	Applicant *Ref.*
The court at which your case is being heard	**Respondent** *Ref.*

You must
- give details of service of the application on each of the other parties
- give details of service on the mortgagee or landlord of the dwelling-house (if appropriate)
- file this form with the court on or before the first Directions Appointment or Hearing of the Proceedings

You should   if the person's solicitor was served, give his or her name and address

You must indicate   the manner, date, time and place of service
or where service was effected by post, the date, time and place of posting

Name and address of person served	Means of identification of person, and how, when and where served	Prescribed forms served

I have served the [application] [Notice of Proceedings] as stated above.
I am the [applicant] [solicitor for the applicant] [other] *(state)*

Signed: Date:

FL415 Statement of Service

Appendix 1   211

In the

Case Number

Notice to Mortgagees and Landlords
Family Law Act 1996

	Applicant
	Ref.
	Respondent
	Ref

Notice to

concerning the dwelling-house at

Take Notice that an [application] [order] has been made in proceedings under the Family Law Act 1996 which affects the occupation of the above dwelling-house and the payment of the [mortgage] [rent] thereon.
[A copy of the order is attached.]

[The next hearing is at

on   at   [am] [pm]]

What you may do next

If either the applicant or respondent has matrimonial home rights:
you may apply to be made a party to these proceedings if you wish to do so.

If neither the applicant nor the respondent has matrimonial home rights, or you do not wish to be made a party:
you may make representations to the court about these proceedings.
This should be done in writing to the court where the proceedings are taking place.
If you write to a county court or the High Court, your letter should be addressed to The Court Manager. If you write to a magistrates' court your letter should be addressed to the Clerk to the Justices.

Signed

Date

FL416 Notice to Mortgagees / Landlords

212 APPENDIX 1

In the

Case Number

Transfer of Proceedings to [the High Court] [a county court] [a family proceedings court]
Family Law Act 1996

Applicant
Ref.
Respondent
Ref.

The Court orders that these proceedings be transferred to the

[High Court] [County Court] [Family Proceedings Court]

because

The next [hearing] [directions appointment] is

at

on   at   [am] [pm]

Please address all future correspondence to

Ordered by   [Mr] [Mrs] Justice

[His] [Her] Honour Judge

[Deputy] District Judge [of the Family Division]

Justice[s] of the Peace

[Assistant] Recorder

Clerk of the Court

on

FL417 Transfer of Proceedings

Form N16

Injunction Order

Between .... Plaintiff
                                                    Applicant
                                                    Petitioner

and .... Defendant
                                                    Respondent

In the .... **County Court**

Case No.   *Always quote this*

Plaintiff's Ref.

Defendant's Ref.

For completion by the court
Issued on   199

Seal

To (1)

of (2)

If you do not obey this order you will be guilty of contempt of court and you may be sent to prison

(1) The name of the person the order is directed to

On the   of   199   the court considered an application for an injunction

The Court ordered that (1)

is forbidden (whether by himself or by instructing or encouraging any other person) (2)

until this application is heard or otherwise disposed of to:

(2) The address of the person the order is directed to

(3) The terms of the restraining order. If the defendant is a limited company, delete the words in brackets and insert "whether by its servants, agents, officers or otherwise"

This order shall remain in force until (the   of   199   at   o'clock
unless before then it is revoked by a) further order of the court

And it is ordered that (1)

shall (4)

(4) The terms of any orders requiring acts to be done

(5) Enter time (and place) as ordered

on or before (5)

It is further ordered that (6)

(6) The terms of any other orders costs etc.

(7) Use when the order is temporary or ex parte otherwise delete

Notice of further hearing (7)

The court will re-consider the application and whether the order should continue at a further hearing at

on   the   day of   199   at   o'clock

If you do not attend at the time shown the court may make an injunction order in your absence

(8) Delete if order made on notice

You are entitled to apply to the court to re-consider the order before that day (8)

If you do not understand anything in this order you should go to a Solicitor, Legal Advice Centre or a Citizens' Advice Bureau

The court office at

is open between 10 am and 4 pm Mon - Fri. When corresponding with the court, please address all forms and letters to the Chief Clerk and quote the case number.

N16 General form of injunction for interlocutory application or originating application under Order 47 rule 8(2)   MCR 073945/1839497 360 3/91 DTP5

Appendix 1

Injunction Order – Record of Hearing   Case No. ....

On .... the .... day of .... 199 ....
Before (H   Honour) (District) Judge ....
The court was sitting at ....
....

The   ☐ Plaintiff   ☐ Applicant   ☐ Petitioner (Name) ....
was   ☐ represented by Counsel
      ☐ represented by a Solicitor
      ☐ in person
The   ☐ Defendant   ☐ Respondent   (Name) ....
was   ☐ represented by Counsel
      ☐ represented by a Solicitor
      ☐ in person
      ☐ did not appear having been given notice of this hearing
      ☐ not given notice of this hearing

The court read the affidavit(s) of

☐ the Plaintiff/Applicant/Petitioner   sworn on ....
☐ the Defendant/Respondent   sworn on ....
And of .... sworn on ....
....

The court heard spoken evidence on oath from
....
....

The Plaintiff(Applicant/Petitioner) gave an undertaking (through his counsel or solicitor) promising to pay an damages ordered by the court if it later decides that the Defendant/Respondent has suffered loss or damage as result of this order*

* Delete this paragraph if the court does not require the undertaking

Signed _____ Dated _____
              (Judges Clerk)

N16 General form of injunction for interlocutory application or originating application under Order 47 rule 8(2)

© Crown copyright

Application for Injunction (General Form)

		In the
Between	☐ Plaintiff	**County Court**
_____	☐ Applicant	
	☐ Petitioner	Case No. _Always quote this_
and	_(Tick whichever applies)_	
_____	☐ Defendant	Plaintiff's Ref.
	☐ Respondent	Defendant's Ref.

Notes on completion

Tick whichever box applies and specify legislation where appropriate

☐ By application in pending proceedings

☐ Under Statutory provision _____

Seal

(1) Enter the full name of the person making the application

The Plaintiff (Applicant/Petitioner)[1]

applies to the court for an injunction order in the following terms:

(2) Enter the full name of the person the injunction is to be directed to

That the Defendant (Respondent)[2]

(3) Set out here the proposed restraining orders (if the defendant is a limited company delete the wording in brackets and insert "whether by its servants, agents, officers or otherwise")

be forbidden (whether by himself or by instructing or encouraging any other person[3]

(4) Set out here any proposed mandatory orders requiring acts to be done

And that the Defendant(Respondent)[4]

(5) Set out here any further terms asked for including provision for costs

And that[5]

(6) Enter the names of all persons who have sworn affidavits in support of this application

The grounds of this application are set out in the statement(s) of[6] _____ sworn on _____

(7) Enter the names and addresses of all persons upon whom it is intended to serve this application

This (these) sworn statement(s) is (are) served with this application.

This application is to be served upon[7]

(8) Enter the full name and address for service and delete as required

This application is filed by[8]

(the Solicitors for) the Plaintiff (Applicant/Petitioner)

whose address for service is

Signed _____ Dated _____

This section to be completed by the court

* Name and address of the person application is directed to

To*
of
This application will be heard by the (District) Judge
at
on _____ the _____ day of _____ 199__ at _____ o'clock

If you do not attend at the time shown the court may make an injunction order in your absence

If you do not fully understand this application you should go to a Solicitor, Legal Advice Centre or a Citizens' Advice Bureau

The court office at _____

is open between 10am and 4pm Mon - Fri. When corresponding with the court, please address all forms and letters to the Court Manager and quote the case number.

N16A General form of application for injunction Order 13, rule 6(3), Order 49, rule 6B (9.97)   Printed by Satellite Press Limited

APPENDIX 1

Parental Responsibility Agreement

Section 4(1)(b) Children Act 1989

Read the notes on the other side
before you make this agreement.

Keep this form in a safe place

Date recorded at The Principal Registry of the Family Division

This is a Parental Responsibility Agreement regarding

the Child Name

Boy or Girl   Date of birth   Date of 18th birthday

Between
the Mother Name

Address

and the Father Name

Address

We declare that we are the mother and father of the above child and we agree that the child's father shall have parental responsibility for the child (in addition to the mother having parental responsibility).

Signed (**Mother**)   Signed (**Father**)

Date   Date

Certificate of witness

The following evidence of identity was produced by the person signing above:

The following evidence of identity was produced by the person signing above:

Signed in the presence of:
Name of witness

Signed in the presence of:
Name of witness

Address   Address

Signature of Witness   Signature of Witness

[A Justice of the Peace] [Justices' Clerk]
[An Officer of the Court authorised by the judge to administer oaths]

[A Justice of the Peace] [Justices' Clerk]
[An Officer of the Court authorised by the judge to administer oaths]

C(PRA)(M) (11.94) Printed by Satellite Press Limited

Notes about the Parental Responsibility Agreement

Read these notes before you make the agreement.

About the Parental Responsibility Agreement

The making of this agreement will affect the legal position of the mother and the father. You should both seek legal advice before you make the Agreement. You can obtain the name and address of a solicitor from the Children Panel (071 242 1222) or from
- your local family proceedings court, or county court
- a Citizens Advice Bureau
- a Law Centre
- a local library.

You may be eligible for legal aid.

When you fill in the Agreement

Please use black ink (the Agreement will be copied). Put the name of one child only. If the father is to have parental responsibility for more than one child, fill in a separate form for each child. **Do not sign the Agreement.**

When you have filled in the Agreement

Take it to a local family proceedings court, or county court, or the Principal Registry of the Family Division (the address is below).

A justice of the peace, a justices' clerk, or a court official who is authorised by the judge to administer oaths, will witness your signature and he or she will sign the certificate of the witness.

To the mother: When you make the declaration you will have to prove that you are the child's mother so take to the court the child's full birth certificate.
You will also need evidence of your identity showing a photograph and signature (for example, a photocard, official pass or passport).

To the father: You will need evidence of your identity showing a photograph and signature (for example, a photocard, official pass or passport).

When the Certificate has been signed and witnessed

Make 2 copies of the other side of this form. You do not need to copy these notes.

Take, or send, this form and the copies to The Principal Registry of the Family Division, Somerset House, Strand, London WC2R 1LP.

The Registry will record the Agreement and keep this form. The copies will be stamped and sent back to each parent at the address on the Agreement. The Agreement will not take effect until it has been received and recorded at the Principal Registry of the Family Division.

Ending the Agreement

Once a parental responsibility agreement has been made it can only end
- by an order of the court made on the application of any person who has parental responsibility for the child
- by an order of the court made on the application of the child with leave of the court
- when the child reaches the age of 18.

C(PRA) (Notes)

Appendix 2

Checklist for Part 1—Property Disputes

1. Check the title deeds. If the beneficial interests are not expressly declared, check the conveyancing file, if available.
2. Does the other party agree your client's interest in the property and/or a sale of the property?
3. If the only dispute is about a sale of the property, consider the criteria under section 15 of the Trusts of Land and Appointment of Trustees Act 1996 and particularly the underlying purpose of the trust. If the underlying purpose of the trust has come to an end, and it is otherwise appropriate, proceed to issue an application for an order for sale—see Part I, Section A.
4. If there is a dispute about your client's interest in the property:
    Is there any evidence of any agreement, arrangement or understanding between the parties that they would share the beneficial interest?
      If yes, has your client acted to his or her detriment?
        If yes, proceed to issue an application based on a constructive trust—see Part I, Section A
      If no, has your client made direct financial contributions to the purchase?
        If yes, proceed to issue an application based on a resulting trust—see Part I, Section A.
    If there is no evidence of an agreement but your client has acted to his or her detriment, has he or she been encouraged by the owner or someone acting on his or her behalf to believe that he or she has an interest or would acquire one?
      If yes, proceed to issue an application based on proprietory estoppel—see Part I, Section A.
5. If you think your client has a good chance of establishing an interest:
    - Find out what contributions of any description he or she has made, e.g. looking after the home, looking after the children, as well as all financial payments whether or not they went directly to the purchase—for the purposes of apportioning the interests.
    - Protect your client's interest pending a decision by the court by seeking the appointment of a second trustee and/or by registering a restriction, notice or caution on registered land or a pending land action on unregistered land.
6. If your client does not have a beneficial interest, what right does he or she have to occupy? Has a notice terminating a licence been served? Is there any evidence of an agreement for which your client gave valuable consideration? If yes, consider an application for a declaration that the licence has not been terminated—Part I, Section B.

    Was your client induced by the owner to believe that he or she had a right to occupy and acted to his or her detriment relying on that inducement? If yes, issue an application based on proprietory estoppel—Part I, Section A.
7. If your client was engaged to the cohabitant at any time, have fewer than three years expired since the engagement was terminated? If yes and your client is seeking to establish an interest, consider an application under section 17 of the Married Women's Property Act—Section C.
8. If you do not think that your client has a claim for a beneficial interest, are there any children of the relationship? If yes, consider an application under Schedule 1 to the Children Act 1989—Section E.

APPENDIX 3

Flow charts

1. Flow chart for Beneficial Interests
2. Flow chart for Occupational Orders under Part IV of the Family Law Act 1996

Beneficial Interests

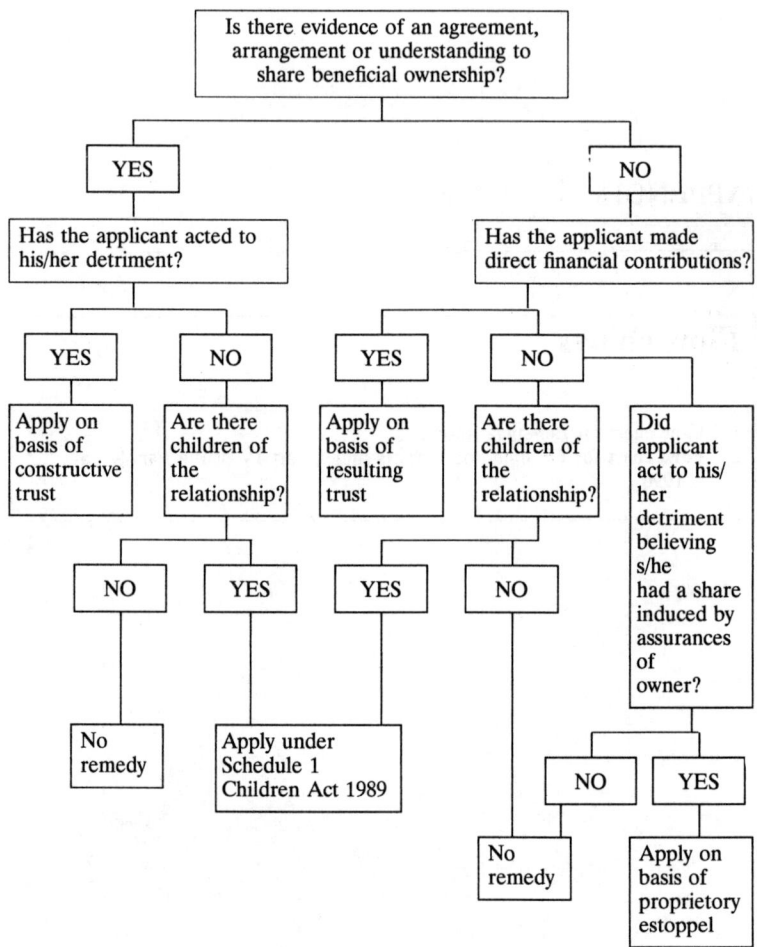

APPENDIX 3   225

Occupation Orders under Part IV of the Family Law Act 1996

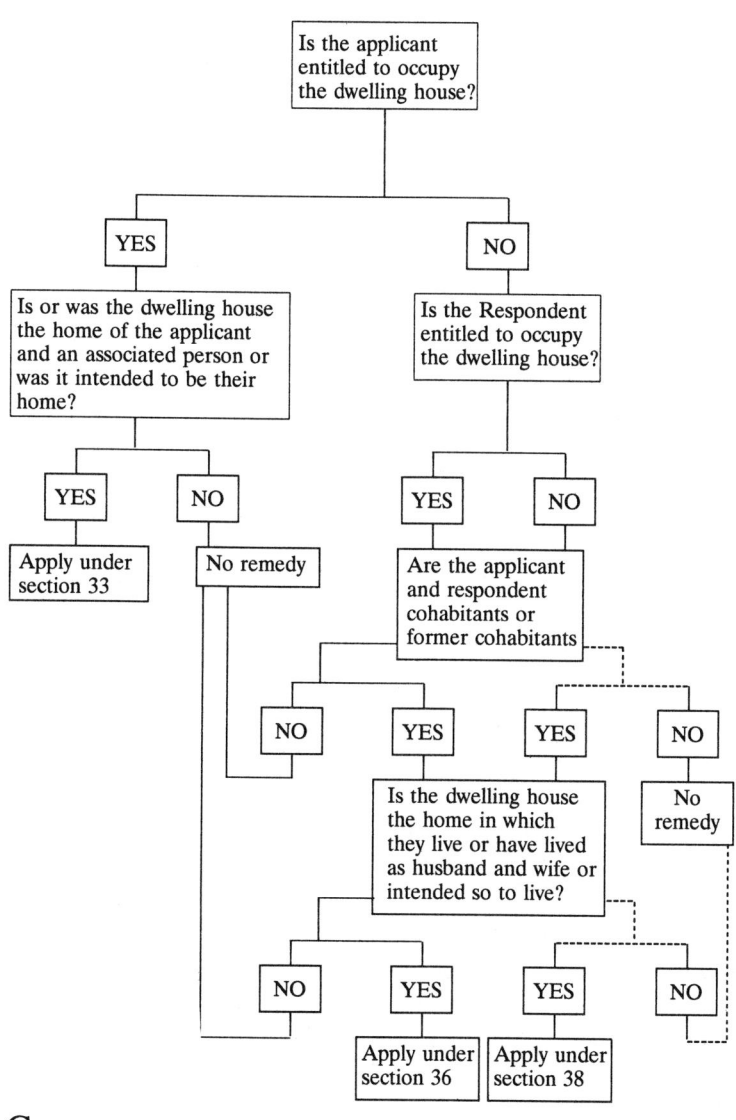

CRITERIA

Section 33
Entitled applicant
associated person
s.33(6)(a)to(d)
s.33(7)

Section 36
Entitled respondent
cohabitants or former
cohabitants
s.36(6)(a)to(j)
s.36(7)and(8)

Section 38
Neither entitled
cohabitants or former
cohabitants
s.38(4)(a)to(d)
s.38(5)

INDEX

References containing roman numerals refer to the respective Parts of the book

ADOPTED CHILDREN'S REGISTER, 3–32
ADOPTION ORDER
 abridged, III–F7
 agreement to an
  dispensation with, 3–29
   notice of intention to apply for, III–F4
  precedent, III–F2
 appendix to, III–F7
 application for an
  directions, 3–31
  jurisdiction, 3–28
  law as to, 3–27
  notice of hearing, III–F3
  originating application, by, III–F1, 3–29
  originating summons, by, III–F1, 3–29
  pleadings, 3–29
  service, 3–30
  procedure, 3–28—3–32
  statement of facts, III–F5
 interim, III–F6
 terms and conditions of an, 3–32
AFFIDAVIT
 application for an order for sale
  replying to, I–A4, 1–09
  supporting, I–A3, 1–09
 application to ascertain tenant
  supporting, II–B2
 application for warrant of arrest
  supporting, IV–A8
 declaration of beneficial ownership and order for sale
  replying to, I–A6, 1–09
  supporting, I–A5, 1–09

AFFIDAVIT—*cont.*
 Inheritance Act claim
  replying to, II–A3, 2–04
  supporting, II–A2, 2–04
 injunction application
  supporting, IV–B2, 4–36
 Married Women's Property Act, application under
  replying to, I–C3, 1–21—1–22
  supporting, I–C2, 1–21
 non-molestation order, application for
  supporting, IV–A2
ASSIGNMENT OF TENANCY
 landlord's consent, with
  precedent for, V–C

BENEFICIAL INTERESTS
 declaration of contents, in summons for, I–A11
 deposit account, in summons for, I–A11
BENEFICIAL INTERESTS IN LAND
 declaration of
  affidavit
   replying to, I–A6, 1–09
   supporting, I–A5, 1–09
  application for I–03, 1–04, 1–09
  directions 1–12—1–13
  notice
   third party, A–07
  service, 1–11
  surviving cohabitee, by, 2–12
  making of, 1–13
  order of, I–A9, 1–13
  originating summons for, I–A1

227

228 INDEX

BENEFICIAL INTERESTS IN LAND
    —cont.
  intention requirement, 1–05
  notice
    judgment, of
      third party, to a, I–A10
    registered land, where, 1–03,
      1–07
  regulation of, 1–02
  title documents, where not
    expressed in, 1–03
  unregistered land, where, 1–07

CHILD SUPPORT ACT, 1991
  applications under the,
    3–01—3–06
    directions, 3–05
    jurisdiction, 3–02
    order as to, 3–06
    provisions, 3–01
    service, 3–04
    writing, in, 3–03
  financial provision,
    application under the, 3–34
    procedure, 3–35—3–39
CHILDREN
  adoption order
    application for an, 3–27—3–32
    directions, 3–32
    jurisdiction, 3–29
    law as to, 3–27
    pleadings, 3–30
      service, 3–31
    procedure, 3–28
    terms and conditions of, 3–33
  contact order as to, 3–17
  financial provision for
    application for
      Child Support Act, under
        the, 3–34
      Children Act, under the,
        3–33
      directions, 3–38
      jurisdiction, 3–35
      pleadings, 3–36
        service of, 3–37
      procedure, 3–35—3–39
    law as to, 3–33—3–34
    orders as to, 3–39
  name, application to change,
    3–25—3–26
    change of precedent to, V–D

CHILDREN—cont.
  parental responsibility
    orders for
      application for
        directions, 3–11
        jurisdiction, 3–08
        law as to, 3–07
        pleadings, 3–09
        procedure, 3–08—3–12
        service, 3–10
    conferral of, 3–12
  paternity
    dispute resolution about,
      3–01—3–06
    declaration, 3–06
    directions, 3–05
    jurisdiction, 3–02
    law as to, 3–01
    orders as to, 3–06
    pleadings, 3–03
      precedents, III–A1—A3
    procedure, 3–02—3–06
    service, 3–04
  prohibited steps order as to,
    3–19, 3–25
  protection from domestic
    violence of, 4–24
    application for 4–10
  remove from the U.K.
    application to, 3–25—3–26
  residence order as to, 3–16, 3–25
  specific issue orders as to, 3–18,
    3–25
CHILDREN ACT, 1989
  actions relating to property
    under the
      directions, 1–32
      jurisdiction, 1–30
      orders, 1–33
      pleadings, 1–31
      procedure, 1–30—1–33
      provisions as to, 1–29
  financial provision
    application under the, 3–33
      procedure, 3–35—3–39
  section 8 application
    contact order, for, 3–17
    directions, 3–23
    jurisdiction, 3–20
    order as to, 3–24
    pleadings, 3–21
      service of, 3–22
    procedure, 3–20—3–24
    prohibited steps order, for,
      3–19

CHILDREN ACT, 1989—*cont.*
  section 8 application—*cont.*
    provisions as to, 3–16—3–19
    residence order, for, 3–16
    specific issue order, for, 3–18
CO-OWNERSHIP
  joint
    beneficial interests where, 1–01
    quantifying the shares, 1–06
  protective measures, 1–07
COHABITATION CONTRACTS
  application to enforce
    directions, 1–27
    jurisdiction, 1–25
    law as to, 1–24
    pleadings, 1–26
    procedure, 1–25—1–28
  breach of
    injunction to restrain, I–D1, 1–28
    relief consequent upon, 1–26, 1–28
  enforcement action
    defence, I–D2
    statement of claim, I–D1
  order to enforce, 1–28
  specific performance of, I–D1, I–D5, 1–24, 1–28
COHABITANT
  domestic violence of
    protection from, 4–01—4–38
  harassment of
    protection from, 4–34—4–42
  same sex, of the
    Inheritance (Provision for Family and Dependants) Act
      claims, 2–01
    no joint adoption application for, 3–27
    protection from domestic violence of, 4–01, 4–34
  surviving
    beneficial interest in land
      application for declaration of 2–12
    children of, as to, 2–01
    circumstances to be considered, 2–02
    Fatal Accidents Act 1976
      applications, 2–02—2–24
    financial provisions for a, 2–06

COHABITANT—*cont.*
  surviving—*cont.*
    Inheritance (Provision for Family and Dependants) Act
      claims, 2–01—2–06
    living as husband/wife, meaning of, 2–01
    sale of land
      application for order for, 2–12
    same sex, of the, 2–01
    wholly/partly maintained, meaning of, 2–01
    transfer of tenancies to, 4–20—4–22
CONTACT ORDER
  application for a, 3–17
  procedure, 3–20—3–24
CONTENTS
  beneficial interest in
    summons for declaration of, I–A11
COUNTY COURT
  possession, claim for, I–B2
COVENANTS
  cohabitation contracts, in
    action to enforce
      defence, I–D2
      statement of claim, I–D1
  Separation deeds, in
    action to enforce
      defence, I–D4
      statement of claim, I–D3
  specific performance of
    precedent for, I–D5
CRIMINAL INJURIES COMPENSATION SCHEME
  application under, V–F

DEED OF SEPARATION
  covenants in
    action to enforce
      defence, I–D4
    precedent for, V–A
    specific performance of
      precedent for, I–D5
DEPOSIT ACCOUNT
  beneficial interest in
    summons for declaration of, I–A11
DNA TESTING
  discretionary powers of, 3–01

230 INDEX

DOMESTIC VIOLENCE, PROTECTION FROM
application for
affidavit supporting, IV–A2
children, by 4–10
cohabitants, by, 4–01—4–09
single sex, 4–01, 4–34
engaged people, by, 4–04, 4–11
precedent, IV—A1
statement of service form, IV–A3
tort, in, 4–34—4–38
injunction, for an, 4–36, 4–38
jurisdiction, 4–35
order forbidding, 4–38
particulars of claim, IV–B1
pleadings, 4–36
service, 4–37, 4–38
procedure, 4–35—4–38
undertaking
acceptable, 4–38
vary/extend/discharge, form to, IV–A5
children, of, 4–24
Family Law Act, under the 4–01—4–33
non-molestation order, by, 4–01—4–02, 4–31—4–32, 4–34
arrest powers, 4–14—4–19, 4–33
ex parte, 4–12
occupation order, by, 4–01, 4–03, 4–31—4–32
arrest powers in, 4–14—4–19, 4–33
ex parte, 4–12
procedure, 4–25—4–33
protection from harassment, 4–39—4–42
transfer of tenancies to cohabitee, 4–20—4–22
undertakings, by, 4–13

ENGAGED PEOPLE
protection from domestic violence of
application for, 4–11

FAMILY LAW ACT, 1996
protection from domestic violence
applicant having an interest, 4–04
applicant not entitled to occupy, 4–06
application for,
affidavit to, IV–A2
precedent, IV–A1
association, where, 4–05
children, of, 4–24
applications, 4–10
cohabitants not entitled to occupy, 4–07
directions, 4–30
engaged people, applications by, 4–11
generally, 4–01, 4–09
jurisdiction, 4–26
non-molestation order, 4–02, 4–31—4–34
ex parte, 4–12
occupation order, 4–03, 4–08, 4–31—4–32
ex parte, 4–12
orders
emergency, 4–32, IV–A13
supplement to, IV–A12
enforcement of, 4–33
exclusion requirement in, 4–32
forms for, IV–A4, IV–A12—A14
interim, 4–32, IV–A14
Part II orders, 4–21—4–22
pleadings, 4–27, 4–28, IV–A1, IV–A2, IV–A8
service of, 4–29, IV–A3
powers of arrest, 4–14—4–19, 4–33, IV–A6
prescribed forms, IV–A3—A7, IV–A9—A14
procedure, 4–25—4–33
transfer of proceedings, form for, IV–A11
transfer of tenancies, 4–20—4–22
transitional provisions, 4–23
undertakings, 4–13
warrant application form, IV–A7
provisions, 4–01—4–24

FAMILY LAW REFORM ACT, 1987
   applications under the,
      3–01—3–06
   declaration, III–A3, 3–06
   directions, 3–05
   jurisdiction, 3–02
   petition, III–A1, 3–03
      affidavit supporting, III–A2,
         3–03
   pleadings, 3–03
   service, 3–04
   provisions, 3–01
FATAL ACCIDENTS ACT, 1976
   applications under the,
      2–20—2–24
   directions, 2–23
   order as to, 2–24
   pleadings, 2–22
   procedure, 2–21—2–24
   jurisdiction, 2–21
   particulars of claim, II–E1
   provisions, 2–20
FINANCIAL PROVISION FOR CHILDREN.
   See CHILDREN

GUARDIANSHIP
   dispute resolution on,
      2–13—2–19
   directions, 2–18
   jurisdiction, 2–15
   order as to, 2–19
   pleadings, 2–16
      service, 2–17
   procedure, 2–14—2–19
   law as to, 2–13

HARASSMENT
   protection from, 4–39—4–42

INHERITANCE (PROVISION FOR
      FAMILY AND DEPENDANTS) ACT,
      1975
   claims
      directions, 2–05
      jurisdiction, 2–03
      pleadings, 2–04
      provisions, 2–01—2–02
      time of, 2–04
   documentary evidence, 2–04
   financial provision, 2–06
   surviving cohabitee, by,
      2–01—2–06

INHERITANCE (PROVISION FOR
      FAMILY AND DEPENDANTS) ACT,
      1975—*cont.*
   orders under the, II–A4—A6,
      2–06
   precedents, II–A1—A6

JOINT OWNERSHIP. *See*
   CO-OWNERSHIP

LICENCEE
   defence denying termination of
      licence by, I–B4
   originating summons for
      declaration by, I–B3

MARRIED WOMEN'S PROPERTY ACT,
      1882
   application under the
      affidavit
         replying to, I–C3, 1–21
         supporting, I–C2, 1–21
      directions, 1–22
      engaged persons, as to, 1–19
      jurisdiction, 1–20
      originating summons, by,
         I–C1, 1–21
      pleadings, 1–21
      procedure, 1–20—1–23
      property, meaning of 1–19
      relief consequent upon, 1–28
   order as to proprietory rights
      under the, I–C4, 1–23
   provisions, 1–19
MINOR INTEREST
   protected
      establishment of, 1–07

NAME
   change of
      application for
         children, of, V–D, 3–25,
            3–36
      precedent for, V–D
NOTICE
   appointment to hear originating
      summons, of, I–A8
   service, 1–11
   declaration of beneficial
      ownership
         application for, on
            judgment, of, I–A10

NOTICE—*cont.*
  declaration of beneficial
    ownership—*cont.*
    application for, on—*cont.*
      third parties, to, I–A7
    judgment, of
      third parties, to, I–A10
    mortgagees and landowners, to
      form of, IV–A10
    order for sale
      application for, on
        judgment, of, I–A10
        third parties, to, I–A7

ORDER
  beneficial ownership, declaring,
    I–A9
  determining tenancy
    death of tenant, on, II–B3
    exclusion, 4–04—4–07,
      4–31—4–32, 4–34
  Family Law Act, under the
    emergency, 4–32, IV–A13
    supplement to, IV–A12
    forms for, IV–A4,
      IV–A12—A14
    interim, 4–32, IV–A14
  Inheritance (Provision for
    Family and Dependants)
    Act, under the, II–A6, 2–06
    extending time, II–A4
    interim, II–A5
  Married Women's Property Act,
    under the, I–C4, 1–23
  non-molestation, 4–02,
    4–31—4–32
    application for, 4–01
      affidavit supporting, IV–A2
      precedent, IV–A1
    discharge of a, 4–19
      application form for, IV–A5
    ex parte, 4–12, 4–15
    power of arrest attached to a,
      4–14—4–19, 4–33
    variation of a, 4–19
      application form for, IV–A5
  occupation, 4–03, 4–08,
    4–31—4–32
    application for an, 4–01
    discharge of an, 4–19
      application form for, IV–A5
    ex parte, 4–12, 4–15
    power of arrest attached to
      an, 4–14—4–19, 4–33

ORDER—*cont.*
  occupation—*cont.*
    variation of an, 4–19
      application form for, IV–A5
  possession, for, I–B5
    making of an, 1–18
    enforcement of, 1–18
  sale of land, for, I–A9
  specific performance, for, I–D5,
    1–24, 1–28
ORIGINATING APPLICATION
  adoption order, for an, III–F1,
    3–29
  declaration of beneficial
    interests, for, I–A2
  affidavit
    replying to, I–A6
    supporting, I–A5
  declaration of proprietary rights
    in property, for, 1–21
  enforcement of proprietary
    rights in property, for, 1–21
  Inheritance (Provisions for
    Family and Dependants)
    Act, 2–04
  order for sale, for, I–A2
  affidavit
    replying to, I–A4
    supporting, I–A3
  service, as to, 1–11, 1–17, 1–21,
    2–04
  succession to private tenancies,
    to resolve, II–B1, 2–10
    affidavit, II–B2
ORIGINATING SUMMONS
  adoption order, for an, III–F1,
    3–29
  declaration by licencee, for, I–B3
  declaration of beneficial
    interests, for, I–A1, I–A5,
    I–A6
  declaration of proprietary rights
    in property, for, 1–21
  enforcement of proprietary
    rights in property, for, 1–21
  Inheritance (Provision for
    Family and Dependants)
    Act, 2–04
    affidavits, II–A2, II–A3
    precedent, II–A1
  Married Women's Property Act,
    under the, 1–21
  affidavit
    replying to, I–C3, 1–21

ORIGINATING SUMMONS—*cont.*
Married Women's Property Act,
under the—*cont.*
affidavit—*cont.*
supporting, I–C2, 1–21
precedent, C1
notice of appointment to hear,
I–A8
order for sale, for, I–A1
affidavit
replying to, I–A4
supporting, I–A3
service, as to 1–11, 1–17, 1–21,
2–04
OVERRIDING INTEREST
establishment of, 1–07

PARENTAL RESPONSIBILITY
AGREEMENT
discharge of. *See* PARENTAL
RESPONSIBILITY ORDERS
precedent. *See* APPENDIX 1
PARENTAL RESPONSIBILITY ORDERS
application for
directions, 3–11
jurisdiction, 3–08
law as to, 3–07
pleadings, 3–09
service of, 3–10
procedure, 3–08—3–12
conferral of, 3–12
discharge of, application for,
3–13—3–15
PATERNITY. *See* CHILDREN
POSSESSION PROCEEDINGS
county court claim for, I–B2
jurisdiction for, 1–14
law as to, 1–14
order in
enforcement of, 1–18
making of an, 1–18
precedent for, I–B5
pleadings, 1–16
service, 1–17
procedure, 1–15—1–18
summons in, I–B1
PRIVATE TENANCIES
succession to
Housing Act 1988 assured,
where, 2–07
jurisdiction, 2–09
order as to, II–B3, 2–11

PRIVATE TENANCIES—*cont.*
succession to—*cont.*
originating application
to ascertain tenant, II–B1,
2–10
affidavit, II–B2
pleadings, 2–10
Rent Act 1977 tenancies,
where, 2–08
PROHIBITED STEPS ORDER
application for a, 3–19
procedure, 3–20—3–24
PROTECTION FROM HARASSMENT
ACT 1997
applications under, 4–39—4–42

REGISTERED LAND
transfer to joint owners,
where, 1–04
RESIDENCE ORDER
application for a, 3–16
procedure, 3–20—3–24

SALE, ORDER FOR
application for
directions, 1–12—1–13
further, 1–13
guidelines, 1–10
jurisdiction, 1–08
law as to, 1–01—1–07
notice of
third parties, to, I–A7,
I–A10
pleadings, 1–09
procedure, 1–08—1–13
service, 1–11
surviving cohabitee, by, 2–12
contents of
summons for, I–A11
declaration of beneficial
ownership and, I–A9
deposit account, of
summons for, I–A11
form of, 1–13
notice
appointment to hear
originating summons of
I–A8
judgment, of, A10
third party, I–A7, I–A10
originating application for, I–A2
affidavit
replying to, I–A4
supporting, I–A3

SALE, ORDER FOR—*cont.*
  originating summons for, A1
    affidavit
      replying to, I–A4
      supporting, I–A3
    notice of appointment to hear,
      I–A8
    precedent for, I–A9
SALE, TRUST FOR
  power to postpone, 1–02
SEPARATION DEEDS
  application to enforce
    directions, 1–27
    jurisdiction, 1–25
    law as to, 1–24
    pleadings, 1–26
  breach of
    injunction to restrain, I–D3,
      1–28
    relief consequent upon, 1–26,
      1–28
  enforcement action
    defence, I–D4
    statement of claim, I–D3
  order to enforce, 1–28
  specific performance of, I–D3,
    I–D5, 1–24, 1–28
SPECIFIC ISSUE ORDER
  application for a, 3–18
    procedure, 3–20—3–24

SPECIFIC PERFORMANCE
  order for
    precedent, I–D5, 1–24, 1–28
SUMMONS
  possession, for, I–B1

TESTAMENTARY GUARDIAN
  appointment of
    precedent for, V–E
TRANSFER OF PROPERTY
  sole name, into
    precedent for, V–B
TRUST
  constructive, 1–05
  declaration of
    pleadings, in, 1–09
  implied, 1–05
  proprietory estoppel, by, 1–05
  resulting, 1–05
TRUSTEES
  appointment of, 1–02

WARRANT
  application for
    form for, IV–A7
  arrest, of
    form for, IV–A9